Rejection is an inevitability of life and plays a particularly bigger role once you start stepping out and making your dreams into reality. It's not a matter of IF rejection will come, it's a matter of WHEN. What John so succinctly discusses in Always Say Hi will not only empower you to break down those walls, but it will start you on the journey to achieving greater and greater success in your life. Give it a read. You're going to enjoy this!

**Ryan Huff**
Founder of Qualified Apparel
Host of The Qualified Podcast

As an introvert, *Always Say Hi* helped me better understand the power of taking risks, managing the fear that often comes from putting myself out there and the simple power of asking!

**Margo Tirado**
Psychotherapist, Author & TEDX Speaker

John's book is a breakthrough resource for introverts wanting to conquer shyness or rejection. In my work as a coach and mentor to thousands of small business leaders, living unafraid is key to achieving what you were called to do and become in this life. The thoughts and experiences in *Always Say Hi* show us that we all have the power to create beautiful experiences each day by simply saying Hi.

**Kary Oberbrunner**
Author of *Day Job to Dream Job*

Powerful story with useful ways to create connection instantly. I never considered myself an introvert, however I could relate to John's fear of rejection. I believe we all go through insecurity and fear in our own way. I love John's perspectives and insights. He shared in a way that allowed me to see the world through his eyes and learn from his experiences. It's a beautiful journey I would recommend to anyone seeking growth.

**Willow Green**
Author of *I'm Sober, Now What*

I am an introvert who struggles to meet new people and John Antonio's book, *Always Say Hi* has given me many ideas of how to break out of my shell and put myself out there. His examples of how he has gotten over his fear of rejection and how he just "goes for it" now are inspiring. He brings home the point that we shouldn't care what others think and our fear of hearing "no" shouldn't hold us back from being social.

**Sharon Kramer**
Chief Kreative Officer
ShadowLight Kreations

*FOREWORD BY JUSTIN SCHENCK*

# ALWAYS SAY HI

## The Introvert's Guide to Overcoming Rejection

## JOHN ANTONIO

*For those who desire social freedom:*
*the ability to create a memorable*
*experience with anyone, anywhere.*

# Contents

# Foreword

Speaking to strangers is never easy and yet so many great things can come from a smile and a simple hi. How different would our society be if we reached out more often, showed interest in people, complimented strangers. Our own lives would be changed, as well, by our experience of giving love to everyone around us. In this book, John encourages you to take that step and cross the barrier of hi, then see the magic that can happen.

In my work through the Growth Now Movement I encourage people to envision what they can grow to become. Change your vision and everything follows. Growing out of rejection is not easy. We all fear it. Stepping out of our comfort zone, which can be as simple as 'saying hi' is the ultimate way to create the life we want for ourselves.

Those of us who are particularly reserved, introverted, or shy may feel it more. And yet this book not only tackles the challenge but shows us our own superpowers - the power of thought. That same thoughtful, introvert can become supremely social and much more when he uses those thoughts to his advantage. We were born with all the tools we need for growth and greatness. We just need someone: a mentor, a book, a podcast, or stranger to show us our opportunities. I'm happy John wrote this book to help you think differently about creating strong relationships.

I look forward to seeing how *Always Say Hi* can empower people to live a life full of beautiful connections. No one should ever feel alone. We all have each other, if we just have the courage to say hi.

Justin Schenck
Host of *The Growth Now Movement*
www.gnmlive.com

# Acknowledgements

Thanks to you, the quiet man. Thank you for being. This book would not be here if you were not. You are magnificent and we would all be forever blessed to spend ten minutes in your presence. The universe is waiting for you, looks for you, wants to hear from you, and is waiting for you to show up unafraid and unashamed. We know you are not a man of many words. Just say that one word though and something new begins.

I thank Olivia, Mary-Therese, Paul, Alexis, Michelle, and Sharon for the encouragement, editing suggestions and feedback during the publication process.

Thanks to Mary and John-Michael for encouraging me to publish this work.

Thanks to Dave Chessen, founder of *Kindlepreneur* and Nathan Barry, founder of *Convertkit* for the design insights.

Thanks to Justin, host of the *Growth Now Movement* for the daily inspiration and encouragement.

Thanks to Pat and Kary, irreplaceable mentors in my development as a person and an author. Thanks to my weekly men's group for telling me the truth, throwing me out of my comfort zone, and never letting me settle in my fears.

Special thanks to David, Vince, Erica, and MJ who shared in my social adventures that contributed to the creation of this book.

# The Beginning

*Every moment free from fear makes man immortal*

— Alexander the Great

When I was sixteen, I left home and learned an important lesson about myself. I assume this happens to most people who move away. They show up to college or their first job and suddenly it hits them that they are gluten intolerant or bad with money. My self-revelation was something like that: I realized I had trouble being social. Now that I was on my own it was something that became more apparent. Sure I was naturally shy, introverted, reserved, but to be honest and to the point, I also often avoided people because I was afraid of rejection.

I was off to boarding school in the footsteps of my older brother to finish my high school education. I stepped off the bus 1900 miles from home. The airport shuttle carried me up a winding driveway lined with trees and I was greeted by a big stone sign that said, "Boarding School Academy." It was the first time I was on my own, completely cut off from social or emotional crutches. It was just me. I had no family around, no friends. This was some time in the '90s so there were no cell phones or social media. The school had one TV, which they turned on for an hour on Sundays to show a documentary. All I had were the people around me: fellow students and the professors.

I was greeted by a warm welcome because the boarding school was pretty cool and minimally cliquish but more

**You can say hi while writing a book**

importantly because my older brother graduated from the same school and he was (and still is) the most popular person in the western hemisphere. Everybody "knew" me because they knew my brother. For a moment I had a crutch again to hold up my social life. People would say, "Oh he's an Antonio," and then make an effort to get to know me.

Within a few days, however, people quickly realized that I wasn't my brother, I was a different person. I was studious, socially selective, and rarely in the moment.

The crutches fell off again, I was just John. I could not ride on my brother's reputation forever. People were still nice but they sat next to me at lunch simply because the seats were assigned. I didn't really have a "circle of friends", I generally found myself talking to max one person at a time.

That was OK. It was who I was, a 3.99 GPA, athletic and academic introvert who studied a year's worth of geometry in the third period breaks in order to make the honors class; who hiked 13 miles of the White Mountain's *Presidential Range* in an afternoon with the help of an orange and a water bottle.

At the time I hoped, however, that I might grow out of it and be able to be a little more social. I will not recount my entire high school experience and I do like short stories so we will fast forward a bit.

After boarding school I joined the Catholic seminary and spent the next couple of decades bouncing between loving people and getting migraines from having to talk to them. I did a lot of things to knock myself out of the shy zone and progressed quite a bit. One summer I even spent entire afternoons at the beach with classmates who annoyed me in order to expand my horizons and not be so socially narrow-minded. By the end of the summer, they actually became good friends. As always, however, I was on the move to new destinations to grab a degree or take on some ministry. I rarely stayed in the same place more than two years. Due to my nomadic habits, for much of my life, meeting new people has not been an option. It has been a necessity.

The biggest move was when I left my seminary lifestyle, an experience I tell in more detail in my first book. Once again I "lost all my friends" while being distant from family. I was living in Sacramento, California where I knew nobody and was starting my first full-time job. I had to build my social life from ground zero in a place I was completely unfamiliar with and in a world that was different from the monastery I lived in before.

At one point in this transition I found myself sitting on the couch on a Friday evening playing *Call of Duty*. Earlier that day, I had two tickets in my pocket for a One Republic concert but no one to go with. At the time, I also didn't have the social energy to go alone so I sold the tickets on social media for a small profit and stayed on the couch creating kill zones for virtual zombies. I loved *Call of Duty* but for some reason, I had a hard time believing it was what God created me for. Aren't we supposed to be hanging out with each other? Man and woman he created, not man and *Call of Duty*.

How do you get over rejection and meet people anywhere when your social network falls away? I have had a truncated, non-traditional path in building social relationships. My friends from the first sixteen years of my life I "lost" when I entered the seminary. Most of my friends from fifteen years of seminary I lost when I left the seminary. I was thirty-one and wondering where everybody was. After that, I continued to move every two years to find my place in the world, land a better job etc. That didn't help either.

I love people. A house full of people is a party and a house that is empty is haunted. Good people change everything. The quiet monastery had taught me not to need people to be happy. But through it I realized that having great people in your life gives you a great opportunity to share love, which is a nice experience. Somehow, having the opportunity to share your happiness with others makes you happier. Maybe that sounds weird, but it is true.

What I was looking for was social freedom. This doesn't mean being free of society. That's called hermitage. Nah, that's not for me. Social freedom, however, sounds liberating. Talk to people whenever you want to. Meet new people whenever you want to. Be happily alone if you want.

Social freedom is the ability to have a social life when your social network is taken away. Maybe they are just unavailable; maybe they got married off; maybe your friends are in jail for dealing meth. In that case you may not only want to meet more people but also meet a *different* genre of people, as well. Social freedom helps you do that. It is like financial freedom, which promises money even if you lose your job or just do not feel like going to work anymore. However, if you gave me a choice between the two, I would probably choose social freedom. Better to have friends than multiple streams of income.

Wait, only one problem. I am an introvert. I have taken the personality assessments a dozen times and I keep coming out as the quiet guy who gets tired around people and does not talk to strangers. When I walk into a room with a head count over five I get anxious. Sound decibels over a comfortable coffee shop seventy-two make me uncomfortable. Or at least these things used to happen. Things are different now.

Today, as I write this introduction I am headed to a fun outdoor bar. I have invited everyone I have met within the past month. Some I met on a train, some of them on the street, a couple in bars. Maybe everybody will show up. Maybe nobody will. It does not really matter. I love everyone I have invited and hope they can come, but if they can't I'll just meet more people at the bar anyway.

There's nothing cutting edge about walking into a noisy bar alone and meeting people. Men have been doing that since the invention of bars. However, it is a long way from being 16, in boarding school, and falling asleep on the window seat of the bus to avoid having a conversation with anyone; and that is the journey I want to tell.

There are many things that contributed to my social conversion. Key among them, however, is the ability to overcome fear of rejection. Sometimes, when I stayed in my castle, I thought I was tired or just needed time alone; but the truth is if everywhere I went I knew I would be well received, I would probably have gone out more. This rejection comes in many forms.

I am afraid of what people think of me, so I stop speaking or at least overthink what I say.

I am afraid of how a stranger will react to me, so I do not approach them.

I am afraid of what people will judge my moves, so I do not dance.

I am afraid of how people will judge my voice, so I do not sing, or at least not outside the shower.

Rejection conditions so many of our opportunities to be social. I was an introvert who had a fear of rejection. I do not think every introvert has a fear of rejection; nor are all people who fear rejection introverts. I do think, though, that introverts can be more susceptible to letting rejection condition or limit their social experiences. One social experience I wanted was to be able to meet people anywhere and anytime. There was only one problem; fear of rejection was standing in the way.

There are many ways to overcome rejection. Some people think that if you just keep getting rejected you will eventually not care anymore. After dozens or hundreds or maybe even thousands of occurrences talking to strangers you stop caring and it becomes natural. You somehow get desensitized to the feeling of rejection or the sound of "no".

Maybe someone has told you, "Just be yourself. Stop caring what people think!" That could be helpful, but it is not as simple as it sounds. What if you are tired or sad, do you just be tired or sad around people? Is that being yourself?

At one point in my life I realized that my social life would vastly improve if I could just conquer this one thing: rejection. Because I live in a city of 4.5 million people and work in hospitals and love the outdoors, all day I am surrounded with people. I realized at one point that every day there were plenty of people all around me that I could meet. There was really no need to download a social app or go on online. Everybody was already right here.

How can a person with an introvert personality combined with social shyness easily get over rejection? That was my question and I found a path. This book is about that path. It is not a treatise on Jungian psychology nor it is it meant to be a precise and exhaustive explanation of the introvert mind. It is simply about a way that works. This way is a path for those who wish to meet more people anywhere, anytime and stop living in fear of social rejection.

# 1

# The Introvert's Superpower Against Rejection

*A man springs from the hidden seeds of thought*

—James Allen, *As a Man Thinketh*

## Hey man, let's go out

In my shy days my friend Jimmy and I used to go to the night-clubs in the evening and talk to people. It was kind of a guy thing, just talk to as many people as you could, young people, older men, women, maybe a few more women than men though. I do not think we were even trying to make friends.

We just wanted to live unafraid of the world. We wanted to do whatever we wanted, talk to whomever we wanted. I enjoyed being out with Jimmy but I have to admit those evenings scared the shit out of me. Being social was a challenge, not something that came naturally to me.

For me, it was hard talking to strangers and each time we went out it did not seem to get easier, at least not at a rate I could have enjoyed. Every month or two I felt like I got over about .3% of my aversion to rejection. At that rate, I would be about sixty years old by the time I could fully overcome fear of social rejection. It took an overwhelming force of courage and determination just to say hi to one person I didn't know.

I didn't have a stash of funny jokes. I didn't have a repertoire of crazy college stories. I wasn't very spontaneous and I was all but comfortable in loud, crowded places. Thinking back, it was almost masochist of me to go to those blaring nightclubs but at the end of the night, we had always had a good time and created at least one or two stories. I live for the stories.

Every time I walked up to someone my armpits would sweat and my hands would shake. It was like diffusing a nuclear warhead. There was no guaranteed outcome. *What's gonna happen? Am I going to do it right?* I want to meet this person but the whole thing could just explode in my face.

There is a certain unpredictability when talking to someone you have never met and know absolutely nothing about. Something amazing could happen or they could tell you to get lost. I think the introvert mind tends to err on the pessimist side and calculate the worst-case scenario and then make that scenario ten thousand times worse. *If I say hi to that person on transit, she will get scared, hit the panic button, alerting the police, and I'll get tossed onto the platform at the next stop; all because I said hi.*

I realized that there must be an easier way to become social. Why is it so hard? Talking to strangers may or may not just be an introvert challenge, but in my experience, it seemed we thinkers had a harder time at it. Being immersed in thought I was more inclined to overthink whether I wanted to talk to someone or not. Then, after talking to them, I'd play the conversation on a mental loop and over-think that too. I would see someone and something like this would happen:

*Ah, I wanna say hi to that person. Ugh, her face looks serious, like she's having a bad day, nah, don't say anything. But then it might make her day if I said hi, ya, say something. Well, she's on her phone, nah. Probably bored, though, and not doing anything important, per-fect opportunity, ya. She has a ring on her wedding finger, would that be weird? Nah, don't talk to her. I'm not trying to go out with her, though; we're just the only two people in this elevator that needs to go twenty-six floors; it actually feels awkward we're not talking, ya, say hi...* And on and on the thoughts went, back and forth like a ping-pong game on double speed.

## Is the hard way the only way?

I realized there must be an easier way to go about the whole thing. If anything in life is hopelessly difficult, you are proba-bly not doing it right or it was never meant to be done. Very few things are never meant to be done, though, and meeting people is not one of them.

I spent several hours of my adolescence working under the car hood with my dad. Probably the first life lesson he taught me was that if the tread is off you don't keep trying to tighten the bolt. You'll screw up the whole engine, no pun intended. Take it out and fit it properly.

God made us to function better than any manmade mechanism of nuts and bolts. Life should glide like a smooth ride in an electric car; if you are pushing your car something is wrong. Cars were not built to be pushed and life was not meant to be dragged.

If simple things like saying hi to a stranger are an experience of medieval torture, then you are probably not approaching it correctly. Take some time to fit your engine bolts correctly. Get your mind, heart, and life in the right place.

I also believe in using your abundant resources to acquire what you want in life. Let's say I had two million dollars and I wanted to become the best boxer in the city. I would not just get the life-fit gym membership and pound on the bag after work. That would be a waste of my time. I would hire a personal trainer to condition every appendage of my body and get my own grain-free sous-chef to feed me power meals. I'd hire the best pro trainer in the world. I would use my abundant resource of money to achieve my goal of becoming a fighter.

Everybody has an abundance of resources in some form or another. I have known people to have a never-ending sense of humor, an inexhaustible mind for new ideas, or a renewable energy for talking sports and current events. Everyone has been given a natural resource or acquired one, the question is how you use it.

For so long, I did not use my God-given resources and I had to overcome rejection the hard way.

I remember the first time I did volunteer work. I had to go door to door knocking on doors and talking to people. That freaked me out a bit.

Since I was the volunteer team leader I also had to be the one to knock and stand in front. The two other volunteers would stand behind me. If you have no choice but to do something you can get over rejection, but that is not fun either and you will probably hate it. Then, at the first opportunity, you will stop doing it. I systematically avoided that volunteer role thereafter.

If you are not enjoying meeting people, the person on the other side might even notice that you are not enjoying it either. Just think, who wants to buy candy bars from a pouty pre-teen who is walking door to door because he *has* to? Forcing yourself is a way to get over rejection. I wonder if it is the best way.

Later, I had a sales job where I had to cold call clients for a couple hours every day. My voice shook like a trailer home in a hurricane. Those phone calls were miserable. Every day I showed up and peered through the sales office glass door and looked at the phone sitting on the desk. Then I would get it together, walk in and start dialing.

I eventually got over it and did it because I *needed the money*. If you need something badly enough you can get over rejection, but that's not fun either. I wanted a better way.

## Show me the introvert way

There are a hundred ways to get over rejection. The question is what would be an easy way for an introvert to get over this fear of meeting new people in random places and then dealing with them saying, "Get lost," ignore them, or just flat out looking the other way. By the way, I've been talking to people for decades and none of those things has ever happened. But what is the nearly unlimited resource that an introvert has that he can use to get over rejection? Many of us may not be naturally funny, spontaneous, or charming. Some of us are naturally good with people, others not. Some of us are good in *certain circumstances* but clam up in others.

However, we, as thinkers, all have one power in common. It is this power that I will speak about until you finish reading this book. When it comes to this power, the introvert is a billionaire. He has unlimited resources. When it comes to this one thing, he can do it better than the other half of the population. And if he can use the power properly he can overcome fear of rejection and many other challenges, as well.

The introvert has thoughts. This is the resource he was born with and can effortlessly create at almost any moment of the day. Asking an introvert to think about something is like asking Spider-Man to throw a web.

**When it comes to this power, the introvert is a billionaire. He has unlimited resources.**

He has thoughts all the time and sometimes too many of them. The untrained introvert thinks when he eats, when he plays, when he is with people or when he is alone. He even thinks as soon as he wakes up in the morning. Other people think too; but the introvert thinks *a lot*. Sometimes the introvert just sits and does literally nothing *but think*. Thoughts are

Thoughts are superpowers

his superpower. He never runs out of them and without them who would he be?

When I was young, it felt like thoughts got in the way of being social. I would be sitting on the bus on the way to a highschool soccer game. My teammates would be talking all over the place about I don't know what. If I did figure out what they were talking about they would switch the conversation topic to something else. Then, I would have to start all over again listening to Kyle list a hundred unremarkable statistics about his favorite major league soccer team, all the while waiting for someone to say something I could relate to. Sometimes I gave up trying and just sat there and thought instead. Then a team member would come up to me.

He'd be like, "Hey dude, everything OK? Watchu doin'?"

"Ah, just thinking, man."

"Watchu thinkin' about, man?"

*A large pizza. If I wanna be a doctor or writer when I graduate. Kimberly from acting class. Which bank I should rob to pay for college.*

"Ah man, nothin," I'd respond. Then I would jump back into a conversation so I could seem social like everybody else.

It seemed like there were social people and then there were thinkers. However, what if I could use thoughts to become social almost effortlessly? Imagine that. The more I think the more social I become.

I decided the days of forcing myself to do stuff were over. Stop mustering the courage, putting yourself out there, gathering energy to go out, and approaching people with inner fear and anxiety. Stop drinking seven vodka tonics to feel comfortable in a crowd. Just stop trying altogether. I'll just do what I do best: I will think. And if I have the right thoughts, the thoughts will do all the work.

I'm not going to force myself to say hi to people in some self-improvement conquer social fears plan. I am not going to force myself to mingle in a loud, crowded room for two hours. However, if my thoughts carry me and do all that for me—OK, I'll accept that.

Imagine if a shy introvert who fears rejection could use his thoughts, something that comes so easy for him, to acquire something that is often difficult for him—social stamina. He could easily make quicker decisions, act without fear of failure, socialize for hours on end, keep up with the bachelor party at the nightclub. What if he could just use thoughts, which come freely, to annihilate the almighty possibility of social rejection, which has been holding him back since he was twelve? He could talk to whomever he wanted and enter any social situation with love and enjoyment.

My journey is about how thoughts changed my social life. I will tell you which thoughts worked and which ones did not. I will show you when I think these thoughts. As a person, I would not describe myself as confident, Alpha, or outgoing. Those are just labels and none of that matters. There is only one thing that matters. Can you control your mind or not? I will show you what happens if you can gain despotic, non-negotiable control over your thoughts for just one day. That is all I propose, and that day could be tomorrow.

It does not matter which color you were born, how you were raised, or what you do for a living. Your struggle with society will always be a struggle with your own thoughts. Master those and anything could happen.

Ok that's enough talk, I'm going to go say Hi to someone, but for the moment try this: make a list of your ten most recurring thoughts. Do they look something like this?

*I wonder what will happen with my career.*
*When am I going to meet someone special?*
*Does this person like me?*
*OMG people who walk slowly drive me nuts.*
*I can't wait till vacation, how many more days?*

Now put a plus or negative sign by each thought. Plus is inspirational. Negative is uncertain, anxious, judgmental, or any feeling that does not create your ideal life. This is not a pass or fail exercise. Just be aware of what you are thinking.

# 2

# Hi World

*As I have loved you, so you must love one another.*

—Jesus

## Hello Universe, my old friend

The first thought we all have is a view of the world. We begin to construct an idea of the world even long before we have an idea of ourselves. From the moment we were born we begin to build impressions of love or fear of the world. It doesn't take a brain scientist or psychotherapist to know that these impressions build with all our childhood and adolescent experiences. We pick up more impressions along the way and they form the view of the world we have today. Our world-view is an idea of how society works, what makes it good or bad and what society thinks of us.

Everyone lives on this planet with a world-view. Sometimes it is complex and sometimes it is simple. If the world actually works the way their view says then their expectations are met. If it does not, then they are disappointed. Some world-views are accurate and others are not.

Sometimes we barely notice we have a world-view; but one area of life where world-views are very apparent and explicit is politics. Take Marxism. Marxism operated on the world-view that society would be better if we could eliminate classes. So Marxist revolutionists taught the poor to hate the rich and engage in class struggle. If they could eliminate the classes, they could eliminate poverty and unjust wages and the world would be a better place.

If the Marxist world-view worked, then Marxist countries would enjoy above average peace and prosperity in comparison to non-Marxist or capitalist countries.

If, however, tens of millions of people died from starvation as political prisoners or simply because they belonged to the wrong class, then Marxism was a failure. It wasn't achieving its goal of making society a better place.

That is a social-political world-view. I give the example because ultimately how you see society influences what type of social person you will become. Every single thought you have about the society you live in will help or hinder you from being social.

You think to yourself, *Society owes me something.* You will wait for people to give you love.

Or, you think, *I am a billionaire with love to spare.* Then, you will give social love to everyone you see.

*Guys in society today just care about sex.* You will avoid men.

*Most women just want rich dudes.* Now, you will feel inferior to everyone who makes more money than you.

*I don't like this city. I can't make any guy friends here* (and it's a city of two million people). Then you will not make any friends there.

*Strangers are unfriendly today, nobody talks.* Then you will not talk to anybody.

We all have an idea of how society works. We have a way we see encounters with people. We can be pessimistic or optimistic. We can be afraid, courageous, full of anxiety or full of love. We can think there are boundaries we have to follow, certain places or times we can talk to people. Or we think there are no boundaries and we can encounter people whenever we want.

We also have an idea of what we ourselves could do to improve our relationship with society.

*I need a better job title; then society will respect me.* And you will not be social until you get a better job.

*I am perfect; I do not need to change.* And you will never change and however your life is now it will stay that way.

Some people think they need looks, money, status, popularity, or personality to become more integrated into society. Some magazines might tell you it is better fashion, labels, style.

*If only I could live in a nice apartment in midtown and not this old studio on the south side of town, I could make more friends.*

I once thought I just needed a different temperament. I took a personality assessment. It said I was an introvert and that I would have a hard time making a lot of friends but still have a few close ones. Is that it? I was just the wrong temperament to be universally social? If I accepted that, then my whole life I would say to myself, "I am an introvert, I am just not the kind of person who talks to a lot of people."

\*\*\*

## *I fought reality and reality won*

Everyone is entitled to how they see themselves and how they see the world. Nobody is here to tell them how to think. Reality, however, is not compelled to respect their world-view. Reality works by its own rules. You cannot change reality's rules. God probably will not change them either.

I once thought that the way I look and dress is what is important. If I bought new clothes I would feel better about myself, so I walked in the store, tossed my card on the register and walked back onto the street looking metro and up to date. Two weeks later, nothing had changed. My social life was the same. That world-view was at least partially wrong, out of touch with reality. Clothe and style alone cannot change my life around. Something more was needed. My view of reality left me disappointed. Sometimes the wrong reality view can even hurt me.

I may believe that arms are good for flying in this world, but I can't force the air to hold me up as I jump off a rooftop. If reality disagrees with my world-view, then my world-view will fail and I will be lying on my front lawn with a broken leg. As I began to explore society, I realized that many of the things I thought about the social world around me were wrong; and that was why I was hurting.

Reality is the ultimate arbiter of ideas. As an introvert I have had to remember that because I have a lot of ideas. I need to decide which ones serve me and which ones do not; which ideas build a better reality and which ones are just out of touch. A bad idea is like a broken toaster in a New York studio apartment: it takes up valuable space and it does not make life any better.

If you are not happy with your reality and your reality is a four-letter word, then the ideas that are building that reality probably aren't any better. This goes for politics, social experiences, or just life. Whether you want to build an airplane or meet more people, your ideas need to be in harmony with the universe.

I once had an idea that I could not run across the street to say hello to someone I wanted to meet, like the CEO of my company, a local comedian I recognized, or a beautiful woman out for a walk. Then I started doing all that and realized the idea was wrong, out of touch with reality. I *could* do it and nothing bad would happen.

Nobody can change reality, not even God. Well, maybe God could, but he generally does not do remakes on his creation because it is already meant to function well. I do not suggest looking for a miracle or an exception to the rules of the universe. Just live with them and be one with them.

One thing that is real is our fundamental social instincts and tendencies. Men will always look for certain qualities in women and women search for others in men. There always be that woman who is drawn to the confident man and man who wants a beautifully elegant woman. Men respect other men who are strong. Women invite the fun girl to the party. Everyone loves givers more than takers. We have social instincts that guide our interactions.

You cannot change desire. If you lobby against nature you will lose. Human nature has been playing the social game for millions of years. You have only been in it for twenty or thirty.

*But I want to believe that going a few weeks without flossing is sexy and cool.* OK, but if reality disagrees with me...

The law of attraction is and always will be the science in which one side is right and the other is wrong. Reality ignores your opinion. If you are upset about your social reality, you may want to revisit your ideas about society. Maybe they are out of touch or detached from society itself. It is hard to enjoy society if you dislike society.

The feminist, the macho, the conservative, the Catholic, the agnostic, the liberal; once they are all on a dating or social networking app, they must all respect the same reality and follow the same data-driven rules of communication, behavior and self-representation, at least if they want to find what they are looking for.

I, too, grew up with a world-view of being social.

It was shaped by books I read, my religion, things people told me I could or could not do. My view of the world was OK but it was not building the life I wanted. I was sitting on the couch playing video games on my night off. What I really wanted was to be spending time with people I had a genuine connection with. I just didn't know where they were or how to find them. Eventually, things started to change.

The turning point in my social life was not when I took the Myers Briggs personality assessment and found out I was INFJ. It was not when I read self-help books full of social techniques. It was simpler than that; it changed when I started to revisit how I thought about society.

## My ideas need to change

Life took a turn for the better when I analyzed, critiqued and reformed my own world-view. I had to change the way I saw things. I had a mediocre way of thinking of the world and so the world gave me mediocre results.

I'd show up to a social and an acquaintance would ask me how I was doing.

I'd respond, "I'm doing OK," which is the sorriest response ever for a piece of God's creation in the prime of his life with a world of possibilities before him. I was living mediocre so life gave me mediocre results.

I was just "good" whenever I met someone new. I was just "doing alright" while on a date. All my social interactions were nothing to scream about because my vision of life was mediocre. I only gave when it was comfortable; I only celebrated when there was a party; I smiled when I was in a good mood; I only loved when I had the feeling, and I spoke to people if they were standing in my comfort zone. It was all a mediocre way of living. There was nothing daring or scary about it, and for that matter, nothing heroic.

Some of the social world-views I am most familiar with happen in church communities. That is a common place where many of us form our ideas of the world. I have been to hundreds of talks given by church and ministry leaders. I think generally religion has improved society by giving us a Divine reason to love and care for one another. And I also think that sometimes religion, or versions of it, do not help us at all. One Faith-focused talk I attended went something like this.

One young lady asks a question. "Being single seems to be popular and fewer people are getting married. Why do you think that is so?"

I'm not going to jump to conclusions, but it is probably safe to say she is single and would like to be with a nice man. Hopefully, she will get some good advice.

The church leader responds, "People today have trouble with commitment..." and continues to explain that lack of commitment is at the center of our flakiness to get married.

The church leader lives with the relationship world-view of commitment. That is, commitment will solve our romantic problems. We need to commit more to each other.

A few of my girl-friends have told me they got married out of commitment—not love. They wanted to do things "the right way" and get married and make a commitment before living together. Now, however, they are divorced. Is commitment really the glue that keeps us together? If it were, there would probably be no divorce.

More than once someone has explained their breakup to me as, "He just wasn't committed," or, "She was flaky, not committed."

It is easy to say our romantic partner is not committed. Our friends or acquaintances are not committed because they did not show up for our birthday. Is commitment really the problem though? In this situation, I cannot say. As a general rule of life, though, I think that if people fall absolutely in love with something they will commit to it. If they are not falling in love with it there is probably a reason. That is what you need to find out. Maybe they are incapable of loving at the moment. Maybe they are scared of loving. It is possible that they just do not love you, and that is OK.

At the end of the day, I might wish society could be more committed so that when I text people to hang out they actually do come out; but I am not sure that world-view does me much good.

It may be true that society lacks commitment. It may be absolutely correct that people who lived two generations ago were way more committed than today's millennials. However, what is true is not always helpful. It took me a while to realize that I cannot control society. I can only control myself. That is an important rule for the social man. It does me almost no good blaming society as the reason why I cannot get what I want.

Imagine telling someone, "You are alone or you are single because other people are not committed." What good does that do? That just digs you deeper into a lifestyle of self-pity, which has never proved to improve any situation.

At another relationship talk a speaker asked the crowd a question. "What do single people today need the most?"

"We need Theology of the Body," shouted a guy from the front row. From his point of view *Theology of the Body* is what we need most. In this, he is referring to a set of teachings from the late Pope John Paul II on the ability of the human body to express a deeper invisible reality and sense of meaning.

If his world-view is correct, then the more books he reads on Theology of the Body and the more such conferences he goes to the better his young-single-professional life will become; he will experience great relationships, he will make more friends and connections and find love by learning Theology of the Body.

I do not know if Theology of the Body will do that. I personally studied Theology for two years and my social life stayed pretty much the same throughout. I have had friends tell me they go to Theology of the Body conferences to meet people but no one ever says they are meeting more people every day because of a Theology of the Body activity. I am not saying something like Theology of the Body or any type of deeper learning is a waste of time. I only ask if it will help you conquer rejection and live unafraid of peoples' reaction to you.

***

## The nice guy world-view

Religious communities back some world-views, but society enforces a few of their own as well. As a man, one of the most common social world-views I have come across is the "nice guy" world-view.

Everybody wants men to be nicer, especially in the wake of inappropriate male behavior in workplaces. They do not want all guys to be nice, just the bad ones. There are actually a lot of nice guys in the world but nobody really cares about them. Unfortunately, bad guys generally don't listen to the nice guy message, only the guys who are already nice guys do. This creates a new type of guy, the Nice Guy (with caps). This guy lives, eats, breathes, and exists to be nice.

The Nice Guy is someone who never goes after what he wants because he is afraid of rejection, being different, or bothering people. Instead of going after what he wants, he is nice to people hoping that they will give him what he wants. It actually sounds nice but for the long term can actually become manipulative. Imagine someone being nice to you just so you will give them something they need: companionship, love, sex, or a ride to the airport.

And then, if you say you won't do it, the Nice Guy can get upset. Generally, we do not want to hang out with people who are nice just to get something. The end result is that the Nice Guy spends a lot of time alone.

While it is true that society helps build the Nice Guy by hammering its "be nice" message, it is also true that Nice Guys have been growing since the crib. Some guys just grew up with people telling them to be nice.

Mrs. Gold from fifth grade got nervous with the boys jumping out of their seats and trading snacks and talking to people so she gave all the boys participation points for being nice and staying in their seats. The boys who got out of their seats got nothing, so the message was conform, follow the rules and you will be rewarded.

Nobody ever gets a reward for fearlessly pursuing what they want. Quiet Jimmy just managed to trade three gummy bears for an entire box of Lunchables, which takes some skill, but he will get no recognition. You cannot blame Mrs. Gold either; it is just the way our society is built. We reward our little people more for conformity than initiative, courage, and guts.

The man grows up being as nice as possible. He is convinced that if he is nice he will win approval from women or society. Now, in his twenties, thirties, or even early forties, he hinges his social experiences on that principle. Be nice and society will love you. If you meet somebody, talk about nice things like the weather or where they are from. Avoid anything too confrontational. Only talk to people in circumstances that are comfortable, like sanctioned, organized socials. Anything else and you might be bothering them.

Other people continued to tell him to be nice; his mom, his aunt, his girl-friends who got their hearts broken by some not-nice dude. There are parental and social attachment theories behind the Nice Guy, which I won't attempt to explain. It can go deep. It can go way back. The only question I like to ask, though, is does this social world-view actually work for men or for anyone?

It *sounds* like a nice way of operating in the world, but will it make you less afraid to face the world? Is the nice guy indifferent to rejection and courageous in face of uncertainty? That remains to be seen.

## So what is your problem?

I give these examples because I have seen that some of the life solutions floating around offered by spiritual leadership or popularized social trends are not always solutions to the challenges that people have.

If someone needs a job and you offer them free health care, you may be giving them a solution but it is not a solution to the problem they have.

If someone wants to learn how to find someone to go on a date with and you just tell them not to have sex, again, you are offering a solution but not the one for the problem they have.

In my own church community I have observed this to be true. When I talk to young professionals about their social challenges, the responses are very different from some of the world-views I hear proposed as solutions.

"I haven't been on a date in nine months," a girlfriend confides in me as we try to catch up over salsa dancing.

"If I get the courage to ask for someone's number, then I can't even get a text back," says another guy.

I can't totally speak for women, but I know that men struggle socially.

One lady friend told me, "My boyfriend calls me twice a day. He moved to a new city and we do long distance. He doesn't have any guy friends, though, in his new place. I'm all he has."

Most ladies who have gone out with guys from apps know that they will be down to hang almost any night of the week because a lot of men don't have vibrant social networks.

One 2019 study suggested that 22% of millennials say they have no friends. An even greater portion report suffering from loneliness. Would that happen, though, if we fearlessly reached out to each other on a daily basis?

I think dating is a good example of our fear of encountering each other. I once asked a group of young professionals how often they get asked out. The average young lady gets

**Hi World, what's up?**

asked out (in person, not counting apps) about four times a year. The average guy asks out about five young ladies a year. Don't tell me that guy only saw five women the entire year that he would like to ask out. Somebody is holding back and afraid of rejection.

Neither guys nor young ladies go out with someone more than once a month.

"I haven't been on a fun date in like two years," says a girl. "It seems most guys are so boring."

"What's a good reason to get back with an ex?"

"I hang out with this big group of guys who are really nice to me but none of them ever ask me out. Why not?"

"All my friends are married now. What's the best place to meet more single people to hang out with?"

Some people say, "Pray hard and trust and God will send you companionship." I grew up with loving parents but if I ever asked them to tie my shoes for me they would have told me with an incredulous tone of voice, "You do it yourself." It may even be a bit insulting to ask my dad to tie my shoes for me.

I feel like God must say something similar when we ask him perform a miracle for something we are absolutely capable of doing.

We ask God to send companionship but we haven't invited anyone to hang out in over a month.

We beg God to put nice people in our lives but we show up to that monthly social with a scared voice and sad posture while only speaking to people we've met at least twelve times.

Which type of world-view are we giving people? Is it one where they need to wait around and hope? Or is it one where they can take action at any moment of the day?

Are we really doing a young lady a favor by telling her, "Don't worry, the right man will come and appreciate you," when she has not been asked out in six months?

Are we really helping a man by telling him, "You are a really nice person, God is going to put great people in your life," when the most exciting thing he has done in the last two months is to stream a Marvel comic movie?

It is a nice thought, that good things will come, but given your current trajectory, is it the truth? It is harder to say, "You need to change some things." I sometimes wish people had told me earlier in life, "Take charge, man, you can change your situation, you can build a life of adventure tomorrow," rather than telling me I was on the right path and everything would work out.

Somewhere out there, there is a perfect way to see the world. I don't know if anybody on this planet knows it, but as time goes on we all have experiences that clearly define what is not a good world-view.

Even people who are married are constantly reorganizing their relationship world-view. After a few years, they learn that splitting the chores down the middle 50/50 was a bad idea or that hiring a babysitter once a week is a good investment. We are all learning, reforming, and improving our lifestyles. We constantly change the way we see both the friends and strangers in our lives.

At any moment in time we all have bits and pieces of the right world-view, only the Creator sees us all perfectly and knows how we can perfectly see each other. As I reformed my social world-view, I discovered a few principles that help to build a better way of seeing society, people, and my social life.

## A social world-view should work

However, I see the world, that world-view should work for me. A functioning world-view will produce results, the first of which is that I will feel good about my life and the world I live in. A dysfunctional world-view might bring results by chance but it will not produce results as a norm. I can fool reality some of the time but not all of the time.

So before championing an idea about society (or at least while doing so), it would seem that the sensible thing to do is measure what type of results the idea produces.

*Is this way of seeing people helping me to create beautiful experiences with the people I meet? Do those around me who live by this world-view have the type of lives that I aspire to have? Are they surrounded by the type of people I would like to have in my own life?*

A world-view is not meant to nurse our wounded preconceptions of what life is about.

I was ghosted once, so now in my world-view everybody is disappointing.

I tried to be nice once and someone took advantage of it. Now the people in my world-view can't be trusted.

It is not meant to propagate social-political ideas handed down to us by our college professors or the media. A social world-view and a view of what men and women should be should just work. It is as simple as that. The way you see the world should make your life better. It should help you connect with society.

## Continuously critique your world-view

Critique does not mean mistrust or discard. Critiquing does not mean unlearning everything your parents, your church, or your culture may have taught you. Critique means to improve it.

Over the years you have built an opinion. Everyone's opinion of society has some truth. Nobody is completely wrong, but to get closer to the full truth we need to be searching continuously. There are people with the right idea and others with plainly mistaken ideas. However, the only real losers are those who stop seeking and fail to admit that their world-view is imperfect.

"Search, and you will find," (Mt 7:7). Cease to seek and you will no longer find. Give up and there will be some things hidden forever.

Critiquing your world-view means refining it. Love what is true about it, but seek also to change what does not work.

Some people have the idea that a woman should never show a man that she is interested in talking to him. He should just know and approach her.

Some people think men should only talk to women in convenient circumstances, like at organized socials, and never on the street or at a coffee shop.

Some people think men don't really need to pay each other compliments. It's just not a man thing to compliment another guy on his suit or his great work ethic.

I constantly need to ask myself if the assumptions about society that I come across are really true.

If I am consistently striking out, I need to ask myself why. There is nothing wrong with the ball. Something in my swing is probably off.

## *Beware the world-view that puts the blame on other people*

"Men today don't know how to step up to the plate." The problem is men.

"There aren't any women who are real ladies." Women are the cause.

"This girl wouldn't even talk to me, what a b—"

"The culture is too sexual. Dating is ruined."

"I can't live in this community. Everyone in this area of town is materialistic, they just care about money and status."

Placing the blame on others or things outside yourself means that there is nothing you can do to improve your situation. It is easy to say that that partner had issues but harder to look into yourself and ask yourself why you spend so much time with people who "have issues".

It is easy to say that women are flaky but harder to ask yourself why someone may want to flake on you.

Want to meet more people? Everybody else does too. We are all looking for the same thing. So why would other people try to hold you back? The world is not against you.

I once thought I could maybe change the culture or society. Maybe we could build a society where people just loved people for who they were. I eventually learned that changing other people is much more difficult than changing myself; but blaming other people is much easier than changing myself.

The world-view that blames your social or relationship problems on society, feminism, #metoo, chivalry, man-buns or vaping does you no good. Only introspection and a good look into the pond will do you good. Become a narcissist for just a second and take a good look at yourself. Dig deep and unveil yourself or find someone who can reveal you to yourself. Your world-view needs to begin with you, not other people.

## *Your social world-view should help you enjoy life now*

I remember one of the many times I was alone in a new city and having a hard time finding people to spend time with.

"It is hard now but you will see the light at the end of the tunnel," a long-distance family member or friend would say.

"All in God's time." And a few years later, things were still the same.

If God created us with only an 80-year lifespan it's probably unlikely that he would would want us to be miserable until we reached 45 when we finally felt comfortable with ourselves and the world and could enjoy life.

Sometimes the "just wait" advice is true and sometimes it is an excuse for doing things the wrong way and or comfortably persisting in our old ways.

I finally realized that some simple things in life were intensely difficult because I was not doing them correctly. Like if a simple "no" hurt my feelings for two whole hours something was wrong. If I stayed the way I was I would have kept seeing things the wrong way forever and ever and spent valuable energy just recuperating from the sound of "no". I would never have seen the light at the end of the tunnel because I was just going the wrong way.

Your ideas about society and people should work today; make life better today, not in a promised five years from now. Sometimes we need to pass through misery to reach happiness, but we will never arrive at happiness by needlessly throwing ourselves into misery.

I question a social approach that says, "You haven't made any friends or gone out for six months, you are just going through a dry spell. At the right time the right people will come into your life."

Good times need to begin now. Your clock is ticking. Everybody has one, only God's runs forever. If your social experiences are sad while you are in high school they will probably be sad while you are in college. If they are mediocre when you are single they will probably be so while you are married also. You should feel great about your life today, in this instant. There are no promises for tomorrow. Tomorrow does not even exist.

One of the strange things about world-views is that people have been known to persist in them even when they do not work. It took nearly a century of poverty, starvation and people dying from violent causes to realize that socialism did not work and then the Soviet Union finally collapsed. There is something in us that makes us love our own ideas more than we love reality. I do not know exactly what it is, but I know it happens.

I have known people to spend decades of the best years of their life persisting in their ideas about men or women when those ideas at the end of the day make them miserable, frustrated and alone. They tell themselves, "Women today are just not like they used to be. I just need to find the right one." And they keep telling themselves that, and they never find that woman because the problem was never women. The problem was them.

Finally, I believe that your life philosophy should also let you make mistakes. The very moment you take a step forward to reach out to someone you are putting yourself in a position of embarrassment. Saying hi to a stranger is potential rejection.

I learned that the more social you became, the more mistakes you make. You will say the wrong thing, take someone to the wrong place, send them a really lame DM that would not get a response. People will become upset with you for not showing up. You will embarrass yourself enough to be red for days. Enjoy it all. What does not kill you makes a good story.

Keep trying; do not wait for the perfect world-view to live life. You will never understand everything there is to know about relationships and people. But you do not need to know everything to make an attempt. Make a fool of yourself, it is OK. Just do it for the right reason. "We are fools for the sake of Christ," (1 Cor 4:10).

> **You will embarrass yourself enough to be red for days. Enjoy it all. What does not kill you makes a good story.**

## *There are no hidden thoughts*

My world-view is the foundation for all action in the social world. Every single thought about the people around me in some way or another materializes into an action, an attitude, or a feeling. There is no such thing as a hidden thought. Likewise, if I control my thoughts about the world I can control my actions in the world. Unfortunately, many of the thoughts about the world do not help me build the life I want. I need to see which ones work and which ones do not.

My thoughts will determine whether or not I come out of myself to say hello to someone after Sunday church or in a coffee shop. They will dictate my response to rejection, ghosting or adversity. At the end of the day, my social world-view is a view of men, women, society and God and how they all relate.

I learned the power of thoughts late in life. I spent so many years trying to do things differently until I realized I needed to see things differently. All action follows the vision. Fix the vision and the actions follow easily. Create the right thoughts and you will never again have to think of what to say.

Choose the view wisely. Everyone you meet, connect with, and bond with depends on it.

Is your world-view working for you and producing great results? Are you happy with your social life now?

Do you think the world is on your side or against you?

Every morning I wake up to a thought. That thought is my own world-view. Here it is: *The whole world is an awesome place waiting to meet me. I love everyone in it.* That thought becomes an image and the image creates the feeling. The feeling compels me to act and that is the beginning of the social day.

When you wake up tomorrow, find the thought you want to start your day with. Before you encounter the world decide what you think of the world. Change the world by changing your thoughts about it. This is the first step to the social man and it starts before the sun rises.

# 3

# Everyone Is in the Mirror

*If small things have the power to disturb you, then who you think you are is exactly that: small.*

—Eckhart Tolle

## What do I look like?

Once you can wake up and love the world the idea of rejection becomes a little more foreign. You start thinking, *Why would anybody even want to reject me?* And then, at that moment, you realize that it is also important to reform your vision of the "me". Who is the "me"? What kind of person is he?

On one of my travels, I learned I had to determine for myself who I was. I stepped off the city bus and set foot in the city of Dubrovnik, Croatia. It was August, the peak of summer. A glorious burning heat lit up the city and visitors from across the world lined up for tours or wandered the streets. I had two options.

Option one was the *Game of Thrones* tour, a guided walk around the city exploring scenes from the hit series. That was the safe choice. Maybe have some fun, meet other people, learn a thing or two about Daeynerys and dragons, and give a super charge to my fantasy pop culture.

Option two was I could explore on my own and create my own adventure.

I thought about it for about half a second and then chose option two, to go solo and create my own experience. I feel the older I get, the more I tire of following other people's adventures. I want to craft my own idea of fun.

I started my wander through the city, my sandals slapping the cobblestone and my eyes on the lookout for tasty options on the street menus or anything that spelled adventure. As a rule in life, I try to do one thing every day that scares me and one thing every week that's new. When I do that, excitement seems to come out of nowhere because anything can happen once you leave the comfort zone.

At one point I found myself walking alone along the castle walls. Walking towards me was a fashionable young woman with a wide-brimmed hat shading her from the 101 degrees of Croatian sun.

I looked at her and smiled but did not speak to her. Years of social conditioning had taught me not to talk to strangers in deserted alleys, especially women.

*Don't be creepy. You're alone on a narrow street, you'll freak her out.*

Then, as I walked away from her, I began to think for myself.

*Am I really a creep? No. I'm actually a ton of fun. If she hangs out with me today she'll have a great time.*

I was just curious who she was. I turned around and ran back. My sandals must have announced my approach from 100 yards off. If anything my flopping footwear would freak her out. I caught up to her and said hi. After the initial shock of meeting a stranger we managed to chat a bit. I only had a few hours in the city so I got to the point.

"Come with me," I said. "Let's go get some coffee." What a dumb suggestion for the dragon breath afternoon heat broiling us to the medieval streets. I have learned that when you are nervous you say the dumbest things, but that is OK. Apparently, 75% of communication is body language. The words do not matter so much. That is good for introverts because we were never a fan of words anyway.

"Uhh. OK. I guess so," she responded with a thick Romanian accent.

We found a cute alleyway coffee shop and sat down. We became friends that day. We explored the city. It turned out we had a lot in common including a passion for Ducati motorcycles and trekking Europe. We walked along castle walls, breathed the Adriatic ocean, and took photos on the seaside cliff to keep the memories. It was a great time and exciting getting to know someone new. It all happened because I took a small action, a tiny step to encounter someone else.

Our actions are just puppets, it is our thoughts pulling the strings. Our thoughts create the show and the applause. We sometimes wonder why we do not take action. Why can't I just say hi? Why can't I smile and be happier? Maybe it is because I have not been thinking the right thoughts.

I used to think I was afraid of strangers. I realized then that my head was just full of the wrong thoughts.

Confidence is a myth.

Shyness is inconsequential.

It does not matter if I am an introvert, a Myer-Briggs INFJ, or a melancholic.

In my social journey, I learned that none of the above really matters. What really matters is that I create the right thoughts about the world and about myself. The thoughts create feelings and the feeling give me no choice but to act.

I have already discussed the thoughts of the world at length, but the thoughts about myself matter just as much.

What do I see when I look in the mirror? Is it a tired, burned out man ready to quit his corporate position at the first available opportunity? Or is it monster of ambition born yesterday, who eats rejection for breakfast and exhales adventure? How I see myself impacts my life at least as much as how I see the world.

If we see ourselves as evil then we become to the world evil and we are ashamed of our actions.

If we see ourselves as lonely, then all we have to offer the world is loneliness.

If I see myself as a creep, I'll come across as a creep to every person I pass.

Walking around with bad thoughts about myself is like meandering life with cancer inside my head. Maybe I can somewhat function and get few things done but I cannot live like that forever. Those thoughts come: *I am not good at anything. I am not deserving of anything beautiful.* Having thoughts like that, I may as well be bottle-feeding a brain tumor. On the outside, I tell the world I am thriving and that I am doing great. But on the inside there I am with my twelve-ounces of brain tumor milk slowly nourishing a malignant growth of bad thoughts that will take control of my mind and eventually kill me. "First clean the inside of the cup so that the outside also may become clean," (Mt. 23:26).

In social experiences, it is not enough to look or dress the part. That actually matters very little compared to thinking and feeling the part. I must constantly remind myself of who I am or who I want to be. My thoughts about myself influence my social life far more than any cologne or edgy haircut.

This battle for the mind never ends. Physical illness or pain, stressful circumstances, job drama, and a million other things can influence my thoughts about myself; but one thought at a time, one moment at a time, I need to maintain them.

Right now, in this moment, as the bouncer is handing me back my ID and I am about to walk into a busy cocktail lounge, who do I think I am?

I learned with time that thoughts make a much stronger impression than the color of the suit I am wearing or the shape of my dress shoes. It matters more than the type of car keys I leave with the valet. My thoughts matter more than any material impression I could possibly possess. Every social interaction begins with a thought about myself.

**Hey you. Let's have some fun**

Many animals must clean themselves in order to thrive. Dogs lick and clean their hair. Sharks are kept clean by plover fish. Even the viscous and dirty alligators need to get their teeth cleaned by plover birds. We, however, not only need to shower before going out, but we need to clean our thoughts also.

## I create my own presence

For a long time, I thought that human interaction begins with what others think of me. I'm walking into an unfamiliar place.

*Nobody knows me here. I'm going to leave.*
*That clique over there are never really friendly, I'll stay away.*
*This group is full of friends from church, I will be accepted here.*
*That person looks mad. No way I'm talking to him.*

With time I discovered that interpersonal relationships actually begin with what I think of myself and have almost nothing to do with what other people think of me. Most of the time people aren't even thinking about me anyway. I am nobody to the random people who surround me every day. It is what I think about myself that creates my presence among them.

What does your consciousness tell you about yourself? If you love yourself you give other people permission to love you. If you pity yourself then you only invite others to pity you but not to love you. Start respecting yourself and you can imagine what happens.

If you are worried about being creepy then you must think that you are a creep somewhere deep inside. That was part of the lesson I learned in Dubrovnik. Being social is about sharing yourself with others. You are more likely to share yourself, though, if you think you have something good to share.

At the beginning of my social journey, I thought that thoughts were worthless, that it was actions that mattered. Take action, sign up, show up, say hi and so forth.... I constantly challenged myself to take more action. Action is good, but now I see that good action comes much easier when there are good thoughts.

I started to learn that critical self-thinking sabotages self-giving and if I have nothing to give there is no way I can be social. It is never thoughts or actions. It is always thoughts then action. Everything we ourselves do is born from what we think of ourselves.

## I have a history of thoughts

Self-vision begins early in life. Ideally, you might experience plenty of love and appreciation as a child or a teenager. By the time you get to your twenties you have a healthy vision of yourself.

You have spent a couple decades loving yourself and being loved and taking care of yourself. You are healthy and strong, heading towards life's prime.

Sometimes that is missing though. What if someone did not experience much love? Maybe that person just had one real friend and the rest of the world was indifferent. Well, no point in blaming the past or your parents. What is done is done. Life is never perfect nor meant to be. Fortunately, love is not hard to find. Both God and the world are waiting to love you if you let them. Then, if they fall through, you can always just love yourself.

## I set the rules

Self-love is actually not a bad idea because if you do not know what to think of yourself then others will tell you what to think of yourself. They will tell you what you can or cannot do, who you can or cannot be friends with, talk to, date, and the rest. And you will do just that and nothing more.

"Oh, you're not certified? You can't have that job."

"Oh, you're only 5'7? You can only go out with people of a certain height."

"You want to dance on the stage? You have to get drunk first."

But depending on what you think of yourself, you can break all the rules and do what you want.

It is also no secret that the attitude you have towards yourself projects on the attitude you have towards others. Self-perception is key not only to how people treat you but also to how you will treat others. If you cannot even love yourself, then what do you have to offer others? "You shall love your neighbor as yourself," (Mk 12:31). Every social encounter begins with me loving myself.

Sometimes finding things to love about yourself can be hard, but let's break it down. You exist as body and soul. Your body is irremovable from the way you are. Your soul is what gets you out of bed in the morning. Together they are the only reason you are alive and you can do something so simple as smile or eat a donut.

If your body and soul could be considered separate from you, they would be your greatest allies in life. Both the "physical you" and the "soul you" deserve love. They are "on your side". They *are* you. So you are the first being deserving of your own love.

People often wonder who the next person they will "fall in love with" will be or who will be their first friend when they move to a new city. I do not think it is hard to imagine. You just look in the mirror. Who is that person? What is that person like? That will be how your next friend, lover, or relationship will be.

If one day we end up finding ourselves critical of the world, of the opposite sex, of people we find on social apps, it all began somewhere. It probably began with us being too critical of ourselves. Love your own profile first and it will be easier to love others.

People have sometimes asked me, "What was your worst date?" I never have a response; I've loved everyone I've been out with. I loved something special about each of them. It is not hard to do because I have a lot of faults and failings. So if I've been able to love myself despite my imperfections, loving even an annoying experience with someone is not hard and life becomes a whole lot more fun. I have just never been on a bad date. Sure, I have had a first show up and get angry and shout at me, but that does not make it bad. It's just another type of adventure.

Self-appreciation, much like meaning, does not come from the world. It is easy to spend much of your life hoping it would. I certainly did. I hoped the right career or people would drop into my life and make me feel complete. When I look back, however, I see that the journey to having a great image of myself had nothing to do with career promotions, where I was vacationing or whether I made an awesome new friend that day. It began with something much deeper inside.

Love the heck out of society but do not expect anything from it. Don't expect it to make you feel good about yourself. Generally, people in society are not going to make it their life mission to come and nurture you to make you feel good about yourself. Your parents may have played that role when you were young, but now you are on your own. You must create your own feelings just as you must tie your own shoes.

## *I'm feelin' good about me*

There are many barriers to a healthy self-perception. As life happens painful things also happen to us and it is difficult in those moments to maintain positive self-thoughts. We do not always feel great. So many things can bring our mood down: a ghosted date, corporate drama at work, IBS, divorce, allergies, or even a sugar hangover from the midafternoon chocolate binge. You do not feel so good about yourself in those moments and that is a challenge but one you must take up at almost every moment of the day. The social man may not always have mastery over how he feels but he can always master how he *feels about himself.*

It helps to remember that purpose is much deeper than feeling. That was the lesson of the Agony in the Garden in the four Gospels. Jesus is sweating blood in a garden, all alone, thinking about how he is about to die on a cross. He did not feel good.

However, Christ, in his worst, most unproductive moment, sweating blood and crying to God, abandoned by all his friends...even in that moment, he still believed he was the Son of God and no less. You may feel like a banana peel on a dirty street, but your purpose does not change.

Even in his agony and pain and loneliness he always knew that his life was worth something great. Otherwise, he would never have bothered to go beyond the Garden and give it on the cross. Why should He give his life if it were not worth anything?

He could have sailed off to Crete or some Mediterranean island and just enjoyed honey wine and a comfortable life. His life was worth something still. It was worth a lot more than a beach and a glass of wine. So he gave it on the cross. Nobody gives of themselves if they feel useless. You give when you feel rich. You take when you feel empty. Christ gave because he still believed he was the Son of God.

If you are disappointed in yourself there is only one person in the world who can fix that. It is you. I used to think that feeling good about yourself was the work of a lifetime. I don't have a lifetime though. I just have today. I have this moment. Reality is now. The future is theory, the present is real.

The negative comments need to go.

"I'm not popular. None of the cute girls want to go out with me."

"I'm not pretty enough. I get all the weird guys asking me out."

"Nobody gets my sense of humor."

"I'm never invited..."

"I'm always alone."

"I'm invisible."

They are rarely completely true and they are always self-deprecating. Usually, self-deprecation originates in some sort of reality.

The last eight Fridays you have spent *sans* plans with no one to hang out with so now you say your life sucks. And then your life sucks more because you think it sucks. The circle of apparent failure and failed thoughts perpetuates itself.

***

## Time to invent something

How do you, then, create a new cycle? How do you build new memories and a new self-perception when there seems to be so little evidence to support who you want to be? You are not a hero. You are not popular. You are not funny. You struggle to hold a five-minute conversation.

That is a real-life challenge. How do you reinvent yourself? Everybody has to do it. Some people reinvent themselves after high school or college, others after a divorce or breakup. Even celebrities and actors reinvent themselves from time to time and produce movies later in life that are very different from their earlier ones.

Often, reinvention takes time. For some people, reinvention becomes a lifelong battle and they are not truly happy with themselves until several decades into their existence.

Others may learn to revolutionize their self-perception within a few months.

I think there is no reason why it should take more than an hour because now is all you have. You can have a five-year plan to reinvent yourself, but in reality all you have is right now. Youth is passing, time is running away, don't wait.

"Once I get a girlfriend or boyfriend, I will feel good about myself."

"Once I start throwing parties in the new condo I'm going to buy...then I'll feel good."

Reinvent, *right now.* I remember once walking into the cafeteria at work. I had been going to the same cafeteria for years in a half conscious, I'm tired and hungry sort of way. By noon I didn't have much to give, I always sat down there with low energy thinking about work. I came to fill myself up, not to give. I was so focused on my career and the next job I wanted to get. Once I got that job, I would be enjoying life more, become a boss, maybe even start dating. Once my career was in place, I would start socializing and going out more.

I either barely noticed the people in my surroundings or simply did not have the energy to encounter them. I decided one day to change. I wanted to become a different person in the cafeteria.

I was going to love my life and show love even in the middle of the workday. I saw a beautiful young girl having lunch by herself. As much as I tried to focus on my screen of emails while swallowing Thai curry my eyes kept trailing back to her. I imagined myself being social even in this tired moment of the day.

I got up, walked over and talked to her.

"Hi, you're really gorgeous."

She smiled. We exchanged numbers and went to a baseball game a few days later.

It takes a split second to change an attitude and the right attitude will create action. That is all you need, a moment.

There is no, *Once I...* there is just today. How you feel about yourself today is how you will feel about yourself for the rest of your life. The change happens when you decide it happens, not when something cool happens to you.

As you step into the car to drive out into society, leave the radio off for a moment, take a moment, close your eyes and remind yourself of who you are. Otherwise, what is the point? You will spend the whole evening letting people tell you who you are. If they tell you are something great then you will feel great. If they ignore you, you will feel like nobody. Your life will depend on society and that is no way to live.

I remember a time when I used to go to a networking event and if I didn't have any good conversations or if people were cliquish I would finish feeling like I had wasted my time or that society was boring. Now I can say hi to someone on the street, they'll completely ignore me or mumble, "OK," and I will come out feeling on top of the world. I am still the same person because who the world says I am does not matter. The social man loves the world but he does not wait for its approval.

When you know who you are, you also know what you deserve should you go beyond a simple "Hi" and build a relationship of some sort. It is often said that love is blinding. I don't think love is blinding. Love opens your eyes to the people around you. It is *need* that blinds love and nobody needs more than the person who does not think well of himself. He needs the whole world to give him affirmation, something he should be giving himself every morning.

**The social man loves the world but he does not wait for its approval.**

Think of your lowest moment, like when you were going through a divorce or breakup or your favorite candidate got nixed on the bachelor—or is it the bachelorette? I don't know. You *needed* a friend to come over. You *needed* ice cream. You *needed* a flight to Bali. You *needed* to play 19 hours of PlayStation. You become a needy person when you are empty. And you are a prime candidate for trading love to fulfill those needs. You don't want love from people. You just want them to fulfill your needs.

The betrayal of love rarely happens suddenly. People don't generally admit, "I don't love this person but I'm enjoying the company." The betrayal of love happens slowly. It is warm at first. Then we start to tan, which isn't bad either. After a while the skin is burnt and peeling and we look ten years older.

Men sometimes betray love. Most of us at one point have been that guy in a loveless relationship. As the relationship progresses the guy feels proud of himself for finding a stylish, beautiful girlfriend. However, he fails to notice that she rarely responds to his calls and never messages to see how his day is going. He has taken her out a hundred times, but she's never offered to pick him up a coffee. He has made her dinner, but she has never offered to wash a glass. There are no signs of love or appreciation, but she maybe is cute or she has something he needs, so he stays.

Over several months this continues until one day they break up over an argument about who they should be for Halloween. He asks himself why it ended. He thinks back on the relationship with hindsight clarity. Then he realizes there was never love. He had slowly traded love for other things. He had decided he did not really need someone who loved him. He just needed the companionship.

He realizes he was attracted to her in many ways but at the end of the day she never really cared about him. He stayed with her because she fulfilled an insecurity, she made him feel less alone, her beauty made him feel good about himself. Need blinded his ability to sense love. She stayed with him for whatever reason but not for love.

We are always on a search for who we are and what we are good enough for. One of the benefits of believing in a

Christian, loving God and Creator is that it's easy to be good enough for Him. He has pretty low standards considering he let his best friends lie and leave him precisely when he needed them. Being good enough for God is a good foundation for building a healthy self-vision.

I'm not a saint, I occasionally say inappropriate things after a glass of cabernet and I randomly get enough bad thoughts to make Hugh Hefner blush. However, I do believe that I'm good enough for God and I think this is the first step to being good enough for anyone else. If you are good enough for the Creator you are probably good enough for any of his creatures. It is not easy being good enough for God, he asks a lot, but I do my best.

I confess my sins, repent of my mistakes.

I make the best use possible of the talents he has given me.

I put my abilities at the service of others.

I do not judge people.

I dedicate myself to my created purpose.

It is not easy waking up every morning and remembering you are a badass, a hero, or just a great guy. Fortunately, though, it is easier if you spend time with people who do think that about you. That is where your friends come in.

One person who knew this very well was Jesus. One of the first things he did before immersing himself in society was choose twelve friends or apostles. They were not perfect, as mentioned; they were temperamental, undependable, naive and sometimes outright cowards. However, they did leave behind their lives to follow him. They tried to accompany Him as best they knew how.

Christ was much bigger than the world but even He did not want to face it alone. If God wanted to have friends, you need them too. I am not saying go out and "get friends". You can't get friends. You just do things that welcome people into your life and stop making that excuse for yourself about "not being able to make any good friends in this city".

That's ridiculous. Show love to people. Build your adventure. Invite them to accompany you. Ask for nothing and you will see there are amazing people who want to be close to you.

Friends are good. Sometimes they encourage you to greatness and sometimes they just help you see your life through any lens but your own, which is a good thing also. They challenge you. They help you see the bright side.

## Who's that man?

Stop asking yourself, "What am I good enough for? Who can I talk to? Where can I go?" Turn everything into a statement and decide what you want.

Don't walk onto the rooftop bar, looking for the group you were supposed to meet. The whole bar is your group if you decide it is. Believe you are worth meeting. All the people you will become friends with that night are in the mirror.

Is that person hopeful? Is that person beautiful? Happy? Loving? Excited about life?

Whoever that person in the mirror is ... that is the person you will meet tonight. Those are the people who find a way into your life.

And this is the second thought that the social man has as he continues his morning. As he looks in the mirror, straightening his tie and making sure his hair is casually messed up, he thinks to himself, *I am a gift to the world.*

Before he talks to anyone that day, he remembers that. He repeats it to himself. He is walking out the door; he reaches into his pocket but hesitates. Before checking his phone, he checks his thoughts about himself. Suddenly, his relationships with the world is very different. He is not there to take; he comes to give a gift.

# 4

# The Good Guy

*My love is pure, I saw an angel, of that I'm sure.*

—James Blunt

## The good guy never finishes

My whole life I have wanted to be a good guy, but it was not until much later in life that I wanted to conquer fear of rejection. Here I was this good guy and yet when I stopped to think about it, I was extremely afraid of rejection. It was then that I realized that sometimes the "Good Guy" is the one who fears rejection the most, which is a bit of a paradox because we would think that really good people would be unafraid of anything.

The Good Guy I am speaking of is often quiet and polite; he follows the unwritten rules of society and the carved-in-stone rules of religion. He does not get on stage unless he is a band member, he does not sit at the table unless he is invited; he is socially accommodating to make people—and himself—feel comfortable. He is also very attentive to the customs of sexual discretion like don't have sex before marriage—or at least says he is.

The good guy doesn't do anything "bad". When someone floats his name in a conversation, people say, "Oh ya, he's a good guy."

The good guy also has lots of good ideas: "I'd like to meet that person," or "I'd like to see the city under better political leadership." However, he only takes action when it is *comfortable, convenient, or socially acceptable* so he rarely finishes or acts on his ideas.

If this guy is so good, however, why is it that he fears rejection and he is the same guy who will rarely reach out and say hi to someone while walking home from work on Friday or leaving a church on Sunday? You know that guy, maybe you have even been that guy.

The good guy builds his brand on not doing evil; but is "not doing evil" enough to make a really good guy? Or, at least the type of good guy we would all dream of becoming? I found it quite easy to follow the rules and conform. I wonder if that describes a truly good guy or just a scared guy.

It brings to mind something that happened to me during my ministry internship many years ago. I was sitting at dinner with a Spanish family in the community of Sacramento, California. As a Catholic seminarian, I was doing an internship in family and youth ministries. This meant having dinner with families every couple of weeks; a glass of wine, share stories, get to know each other. It was an opportunity to spend quality time with them outside the hectic retreats and community events we organized.

On this occasion, the older son in the family, in his early 30s, had invited a young girl to the dinner. She was a madrileña (someone from Madrid), whom the son appeared to be casually dating. We all mingled together over a glass of wine and then sat down to eat. The madrileña was sitting next to me. I started on my salad, trying to attach the rebellious Romaine leaves to my fork while telling a story.

She was absolutely beautiful standing straight, but now she was leaning in to me, listening intently to the story I was telling. Legs crossed, hanging off the right side of the chair she faced me directly and lazily dangled her arm from its wooden spine.

Across the table, her Spanish boyfriend, man friend, whatever a guy is called at that stage of a relationship, frowned and commented, "Ayyye! Por que te pones tan guapaaa? Te pones muy guapa, eh?!"

I, of course, understood Spanish perfectly well. I understood that in some ways she was showing a little too much interest in me for the comfort of her boyfriend.

The moment was a touch awkward so I just did what I did best in awkward moments: I ignored it and continued with my story.

I tell that story because the incident reminded me that I have opportunities and it made me feel good. In that moment she reminded me that I did not have to be there in seminary, I could be elsewhere, maybe in a nice relationship experiencing great intimacy.

I was a Good Guy not because I was following a rule. I was good because I had an opportunity to break it and I still followed it. It is actually fairly easy not to have sex if you never have the opportunity for sex. I have seen some people follow rules simply because they do not have the strength of will or opportunity to break them.

I tell the story because many men today tend to base their social presence on what they are not doing.

*I'm a good guy, I don't do hookups.*
*I'm honest, I'll never hurt you.*

In light of the #metoo movement and stories of billionaires using their wealth to grab sexual favors, society has a tendency today to produce a sexless man. Some of the men accused in this movement are guilty and it is absolutely good they are brought to light. Then, some have actually been proved innocent and it makes the rest of us think it is better to be nonsexual in every shape or form to keep our careers or reputations from being ruined forty years later.

Being a Catholic, I also jump in and out of church events throughout the year and in that community, sex while dating is generally frowned upon. The Catholic Church makes it a priority to tell people, "Don't have sex."

I'm not about to talk about the appropriate time or place for sex. I simply want to say that before a man decides the appropriate circumstances for sex I think he needs to ask if anyone he's crazy about even wants to have sex with him.

I had been living a vow of chastity for several years in seminary but that evening in Sacramento was the first time I lived a sexual virtue. It was not until I had the opportunity to break the vow that living it became a virtue. Virtues and vows are two very different things. The vow becomes virtue when you have the power and opportunity to break it but refuse to do so.

That gorgeous person staring into my face from the chair next door, smiling, inviting me into her presence; it was a moment of tension, passion, a sign of opportunity. In that moment, I had to make a decision and the decision is the first step to virtue. After all, where is the virtue if there is no danger? Where is the good if there is no capacity for "bad"?

Today my social and dating life is at liberty, maybe a tad libertine, I no longer have a vow not to have sex with anybody. However, whatever rule I choose to live by I have to ask myself if I even have the power to break it if I wanted to.

Some monks in the world take a vow of silence. If you place that monk on an island, however, the vow loses all its power and virtue. What good is a vow of silence when there is no one to talk to? The vow of chastity becomes meaningful when you know there are actually people you could share intimacy with. Saying you follow a rule or commandment always implies that you have the opportunity to do otherwise.

## *To do or not to do...Is it really the question?*

I mention all this because as I journeyed from shy to social I realized that how I feel about sex and my own sexuality has a lot to do with my social attitude. I overcome fear of rejection with power, sexual energy, and love, not by making a list of things I "don't do". When I love the power of my sexuality, I begin to feel that incredible force change my day.

I do not think moral communities (especially religious ones) encourage men to do that. They simply define the *good guy* as the one who doesn't have sex or does not break rules. At some point most men are asked by a nice Christian young lady, "How many women have you been with?" She wants to know if you are a "good guy". Do you get around or are you someone conservative?

Nobody really asks, "How many times have you had the opportunity for loving sex?" They just want to know what you have not done.

This has been my personal experience of Christian communities over the years. A dating talk is generally a chastity talk. A relationship seminar is full of talks on sexual purity. Your ability to wait for sex is what defines you as a man. Many young adult talks are summarized as "don't have sex" or do anything that could lead to sex. Is that what it is really all about? Does no sex actually equal manliness and virtue? Is the good guy in society really the one who does not do frowned upon actions?

I believe that sex is something precious and special, with a time, circumstance and place, but I am not sure that simply not having sex makes you a better man.

If chastity is simply a matter of not having sex then there are actually quite a few people in the world who are living it. A lot of people are not having sex. Loving, passionate, meaningful sex is something hard to come by. I heard some people who are married aren't even having sex; not because they don't want to but because their partner no longer considers them attractive. But are they living sexual virtue, chastity, if you call it that?

## Who is the real good guy?

Let's imagine that somewhere in the world there is an obese five-hour-a-day video gamer sitting on his couch in tighty whities on a Friday night. He is not having sex. So is he one of the good guys? Is he one of the guys that society is proud of?

You can say hi to an entire group of people

Then take the ten-years married start-up entrepreneur, traveling for business. While visiting a distant city a girlfriend from the past invites him to connect at a wine bar. Apparently, she is interested in collaborating with his start-up, offering her marketing services. For this man, chastity means only having sex with his wife, with whom he has made a commitment.

That night, neither man has sex. The gamer only fingers his controls. The entrepreneur has one glass of wine with the college friend. She signals that she misses him, but he goes back to his hotel alone.

Both the entrepreneur and the gamer are clearly not having sex that night so are both equally the good guy?

Most would say the entrepreneur is the good guy. He is inspiring in some sort of way. The gamer is not someone we are going to tell stories about. Why doesn't anyone mention our gamer who has not had a shower in 72 hours as an example of chastity or an example of social virtue?

"Look at that guy, he plays video games every Friday night instead of running around the beer gardens flirting with young women. He has let his health go, he probably couldn't put a decent outfit together if he tried, but he is an example of chastity," says nobody, ever.

The gamer gave up nothing. His only option for the evening was to sit on his couch alone drowning in a virtual world.

What is the difference between the gamer and the entrepreneur? The difference is opportunity. The gamer is not having sex but he also does not have the opportunity for sex. Unless he is a *Call of Duty* world champion earning seven figures, he probably does not have a lot of women in his circle who are attracted to him.

The entrepreneur has the opportunity for sex if he stares into those eyes and orders a second round of Malbec.

In my own Catholic world, who are the examples who come across our news feed? It is the beautiful young Vogue model turned Christian who says she's "waiting for the right man". She has opportunity. She can have sex with whomever she wants. But she waits for what she considers an "appropriate moment".

Nobody creates a chastity promotion pamphlet from a photo of an aging nun on her deathbed. "Be chaste like 92-year-old Sister Ursula!" We promote the virtue with people who have the opportunities to choose and make decisions.

Even in the selection of candidates for the Catholic priesthood, the Catholic Church wants men who can live and be examples of chastity. So to recruit seminarians, the church seeks young, healthy young men with above average social skills and intelligence. The vocation recruiters don't go to the over 60s' online singles forum and ask them to consider giving their lives to God. They want very sexual beings if they are to promote sexual virtue. Virtue is the right use of opportunity.

We talk about the billionaire who drives a Prius and uses his money for charity instead of buying a third yacht. We want to interview the professional athlete who leaves the after-game party early to come home to his wife and kid.

Sex is just an example of how people define themselves by what they do not do. The social man lives by another mentality. He does not conquer rejection by "not doing" but by doing.

Sure, you can "not have sex", but how many of the 25 people you came across today felt loved by you? That is what the social man asks. He does not overcome rejection by following rules. He does so by taking action. His identity is linked to his daring, overwhelming action, not by his conformity.

## *The path of least resistance looks "good"*

If you are not at least capable of vice can you really be living the virtue? An aggressive prizefighter can be safe and harmless because he chooses to be. There are others who are harmless because they are simply too afraid to break a rule or handle confrontation. The first actually choose virtue, the others simply fall into the path of least resistance. Sometimes least resistance appears to be virtue, but I think the two are very different. Great men are rarely walking down the path of least resistance.

I remember my first week moving to Texas. I walked into a saloon, glanced around and went to the bar to order a drink. Apparently, I glanced in the wrong direction because a cowboy came up to my face and tried to start something.

"You looking at me?"

"Nah man, I wasn't looking at you," I responded. In my mind, my conflict avoidance mechanism kicked in and I did not even think about it.

"You were looking at me, weren't you?"

"Nah man, I was looking at the bar."

I avoided a fight but not out of virtue. There was only one option in my mind: conflict avoidance. You are alone in this bar, new to the city, avoid conflict.

Sometime later, I began working out again at a boxing gym. I became fairly good and began fighting guys 40 to 50 lbs. heavier than me. I was competitive enough for the coach to tell me to pull my punches and stop throwing the left hook.

"Just the one-two, John, no uppercuts or hooks."

"John! WTF! I said nooo hooks!"

"Oh. OK, coach." I was never a really good listener.

Around that time I was out having a drink with friends and mixing with people at a whiskey bar. A smartly dressed guy joined my circle. It was apparent he had something to prove and began trolling everything my friends and I said. The insults became annoying and I decided enough was enough.

I stepped towards him, stood in his face and said, "This conversation is over."

"What do you mean it's over? You can't just eeend it," he protested. I could feel the liquor in his breath.

"I just did. It's over."

Our faces were about seven inches apart. I didn't actually anticipate a bar fight. Who really fights in a bar these days? The point is I felt strong and I felt like I didn't have to sit there and listen to his trolling. I had options.

The guy recanted, apologized, and actually began explaining away his insecurities. "I'm here at this bar with this group of people but they're not really my friends, my wife is here but she's ignoring me and this and that, and blah, blah, blah."

In that moment I felt virtuous. I had the power to get what I wanted in any way I wanted, peacefully or not, and I chose what I thought was the better path. I made a decision. I asked for respect and I got it. I did not just fall into a safe course of action of moving to the other end of the bar.

I had the *capability* and that was the difference. That is what makes powerless resignation something different from virtue. The word virtue actually comes from the Latin *vir*. This means "man" in the sweaty, smelly testosterone sense. It sounds like valor, strength, merit, things that come with capability and are completely dissociated from resignation. It is not about what you are not doing. Nobody cares about that.

Make an entire litany of things you don't do: drugs, smoke, binge drink... Post it on your social feed, read it off to someone on your next date, tell the world. Nobody cares. God probably doesn't care either. What really matters is what you *are doing* in the world. In the Parable of the Talents, the man who did nothing with his talent was the only one who was punished (Mt 25:14). Those who took action, took a chance, and invested their talents were rewarded.

There is no virtue without power and power comes from daring, decisive, good but even sometimes unthinkable forms of action. When you talk about your week and someone smiles at you and says, "I can't believe you did that," you know you are probably becoming a person of action.

Moral communities and religious groups want to produce good guys and good people. However, are they creating men of power and opportunity or simply men who can follow rules?

I think a speaker who tells an audience that they are become great people by simply "not-doing" something or not breaking a law is misleading people. Does virtue descend on the powerless and resigned? Or is it the reward of a deliberate, conscious decision? I think virtue grows within those who change the world, not the ones who preserve themselves from harm.

I remember once making it the focus of my social life to avoid having sex and saving myself for someone special. My social life was mediocre. I forgot about the whole sex thing and changed my mission to make people feel loved, old, young, men, women, single, married, whoever. Then life started to change.

People breaking rules is not what is ruining the world, people just taking care of themselves and doing nothing good is what is ruining it. When someone spends an entire day without genuinely caring for anyone, the world falls apart just a little bit more. People being isolated in their own little world and dramas is what is letting it fall apart.

## There's just no sacrifice

The idea of any sexual virtue is that you're "giving up" an opportunity for meaningful sex in the pursuit of some greater good.

By opportunity for sex I don't mean just sex. Most men could afford to pay for the company of someone for at least a few minutes. Most women could have sex tonight with any boring guy from a phone app or free dating site. That is generally not the type of sex that makes us feel great about ourselves. Having sex with someone you are plainly not attracted to but just out of loneliness or boredom is not a real opportunity for sex.

Nobody says, "I've been heroically good this week, I haven't called that escort service." Hey bro, you shouldn't be calling them anyway.

There's only one type of sex that really matters: intimacy with someone you are crazy about and that other person is crazy about you. That is what we crave. And yet very few of us regularly have that opportunity. When was the last time you even had a conversation with someone you were crazy about? Frankly, I don't think a lot of us have that opportunity.

An opportunity like that would consume our emotions; instead, we sell our emotions to the streaming video industry that feeds us drama, adventure and rom-coms and stories of things that never really happened. If we did have those real opportunities I don't think we would have built pornography into an industry with a net worth (by one estimate) capable of feeding *4.8 billion* people a day. We could literally end some world hunger if we stopped watching porn. Live emotionally and sexually fulfilling lives and give your porn money and time to charities instead.

I think there are men and women living on their islands all around us. They have limited opportunities to meet people they would like to get to know, become friends with, or something more. When they do get the opportunity to say hi, they do not. They are chaste perhaps, but the virtue of chastity is beyond their reach because most of them rarely even meet people.

## *I feel sexy and strong*

This section is not meant to be about sex or morality, both things I am pretty unqualified to write about. My only purpose is to show that our attitude towards sex and morality can radically change our social perspective. I certainly do not think it is a good mindset to count your sexual opportunities. Forget about who you want to have sex with or who wants to have sex with you. Don't even worry for a second if you are sexually attractive. I did that briefly once and it was about eight seconds of my life I'll never get back.

When it comes to sex, only one thing matters and it is something that I think few people do. All around me I find people who want to have sex or fall in love with someone so they can get married and have more sex. Everybody, man or woman, also wants to be sexy.

The thing that nobody seems to do is just *feel* sexy. How many times do you look around and see someone and think to yourself, *That person is having a sexy day*? Everyone is just staring into their phones like a genie is going to pop out and give them PowerBall numbers. Maybe someone looks up but they have headphones over their ears with a demeanor that says, "I'm listening to a funeral, please don't bother me."

> Hit stop on your sexy alarm clock. Do some sexy exercise, drink some sexy coffee. Feel sexy walking to the metro stop, and show up at your sexy job.

Here is a thought. Wake up every day feeling sexy. Love your sexuality and all the power, emotions and physical benefits or inconveniences that come with it. Be proud of it. Hit stop on your sexy alarm clock. Do some sexy exercise, drink some sexy coffee. Feel sexy walking to the metro stop, and show up at your sexy job.

It is amazing what can happen if you try living just one day feeling like the sexiest person in the world. Let yourself be filled with sexual energy. Love sex and the idea of having it with someone you are crazy about. Feel the sexy power that God created you to feel and rejection will have no power over you. Sexy is more powerful than rejection. Do you think that someone who feels sexy is worried about some stranger on the street saying no to them?

Do whatever it takes to get that feeling. Some people work out and feel sexy. Some people eat well and feel sexier; maybe you need to do something crazy and adventurous. Maybe being close to God's limitless power and love makes you feel strong and sexy. If losing weight makes you feel sexy, then figure it out. I have a few activities that help me feel sexy or most a man. One is boxing and it was in the ring that I first learned the power of sexy.

At the beginning of my social journey, when I was quiet and afraid, I showed up to a boxing competition at Miami of Ohio University. As is custom, a physician onsite gave me a physical before I stepped into the ring to make sure I was in good health. I noticed she was cute. I had my mind on the fight but even if I wasn't thinking of the fight, I was way too shy to tell a girl to her face that she was cute. *Nah, not going to happen. I'll just tell my friends she's cute.*

She cleared me to fight and I stepped into the ring. I won the fight and suddenly felt really sexy. There is something about mastering a skill well enough to win that makes me feel fully like a man. I felt good. I stepped out of the ring and was back in front of the young resident physician. She started examining my eye coordination and asking me questions to make sure I didn't dislocate my brain in the fight.

"You're really cute," I suddenly said. Wow, that was huge for me, but I said it like it was the easiest thing in the world. No alcohol, no thinking, no nervousness, not even trying. It was the same me and the same her but over a course of a nine and a half minutes from before and after the fight I had conquered a fear I had. I never told attractive women what I thought of them because I was afraid of what they would think if they knew what I was thinking. It was some highly complicated form of fear of rejection. Now I said it because I felt like a sexy, strong man. How long does it take to feel sexy? Maybe a nine-minute fight if you really want to stretch it out.

Don't wait until your wedding day to get that feeling. Make it happen now.

The young resident physician laughed a bit and smiled at me and I moved on to celebrate with my coach and team. I started to realize that there were many areas of my life where I was afraid to tell people what I thought of them but now I knew how to get over that.

Find what makes you feel sexy. Forget about what the world thinks of you, if this girl or guy friend-zoned you. Forget about who does or does not want to have sex with you. So what you've gone an entire year without being kissed and your Cardigan Corgi is your only true friend? Don't bother checking your Instagram to see how many likes your sexy gym pic got. Whether people think you are sexy or not matters absolutely nothing. Just do one thing: start feeling sexy yourself right now in whatever you are doing. If you are at a concert or sitting in traffic, feel sexy and strong.

Nobody will stop you and nobody can ever stop you from feeling or thinking that. Enter society as the sexually charged being you were created to be and you will fear less what anyone can say to you. Love sex and love the idea of having it.

Once you establish your sexy new presence in society, use that energy to do great things, cross bridges you thought too scary and meet the people you want to. Break the rules. You see someone you want to meet on the street staring at their phone? Go ahead, and say hi; see what happens.

You really want to say hi to the person in front of you in line at the cafeteria? Just feel sexy; then talk.

The social person needs to decide what type of good person he or she will become. Is his mission statement not to have sex and to be seen as this "good guy" with a perfect reputation? Or is to offer the world something great that it has never seen before? If he wakes up every morning with the thought of avoiding sex or not breaking rules then I wonder where that thought will take him.

I decided to recreate that feeling from the boxing match every single morning. I decided I would approach society loving and feeling proud of my sexuality and my sexual desires. Fear of rejection became less of an issue. I don't mean that a person needs to actually have sex. That is secondary to the matter. There are actually some people who are having sex but do not feel sexy at all. The important thing is to love every single ounce of your gender, be absolutely proud of it and let the world know it. If you are not showing up to the world feeling like a sexy, strong, energetic man (or woman) then what are you showing up as? A neutered cat?

After that Sacramento dinner my superiors in the seminary limited social exposure. I was not invited to socials were young professionals my age might be present. The danger was "too great". It was too close of a call. What if someone flirted with me and I did give in and had sex with them? Too much of a scandal. What if I fell in love with them and left the seminary? For my superiors, it was too much of a risk. I lost that opportunity to be in society, surrounded by opportunities. I lost the opportunity to make good decisions. I don't complain about that. In every event, God's hand is more powerful than any limitations people can put on us. I'm simply thankful that the experience helped me realize that real virtue carries with it risk, danger, and opportunity.

## *The new good guy*

For my own purposes, I redefined the good guy. He is someone who uses his love for sex and sexuality to do great things.

The good guy does not go around society *trying* to have sex with people. That is the creep.

The good guy does not try not to have sex with people. That is a waste of time and energy.

I don't think the good guy worries about sex. He does not look for it. He does not avoid it. He does not worry about it.

Not doing never helped me on my social journey. I can't become social by saying what I am not doing. For the introvert mind, especially the sensitive one, that can be the temptation, to build his value from passivity: *I am not going to hurt anyone. I am not going to bother anyone. I don't want to "make a big deal" about it...*

I once spent three years defining my virtue by what I was not doing. *I am not breaking any Commandments. I am not doing anything against my church's Catechism.* Life was boring and I was at the point of eating a Tide pod just to feel something.

Sure, focusing on "sexual virtue", if you can call it that, may have had its health and non-child-bearing benefits. But who brags about being 32 and not having any kids? Or who goes out with someone just because they don't have STDs? Aren't we called to be great and do great things?

I changed my focus to be what I am giving to the world and everything changed overnight. It is doing that makes us who we are and it is the attitude of doing that overcomes rejection. The social man loves sex. Love your God-given gift of masculinity or femininity. Do what it takes to feel like the sexiest person in the world: powerful, strong, full of love for whoever is in front of you.

The man who takes action a thousand times and fails a thousand times will kill his fear of rejection much more quickly than the man who spends his thoughts trying to calculate the perfect opportunity to act or avoid making a mistake.

I try to focus on what I'm giving to the world around me. When I walk into a room, how do people feel around me? Reach out, connect and discover the greatness in everyone. Fall in love with the whole world and maybe falling in love with *someone* will be easier.

This is the third thought of the social man: *I feel sexy, strong, and I am here to give the world something it has never seen before.*

When do you have this thought? At every moment of the day that your mind is free. Yes, you officially no longer have time for self-pity or social media scrolling. You barely have time or the desire to check your text messages because you feel sexy and strong.

# 5

# I Saw the Sign

*What's that supposed to mean? A wolf's head on a stick. Big wolf barbecue tonight? Bring your own wolf?*

—Eoin Colfer, *The Lost Colony*

## Lord, give me a sign

I sometimes used to wonder if people wanted to meet me. Wouldn't it be great if there were a way of knowing who wanted to talk to you and who would look the other way? I used to look for signs always. I could tell a dozen stories of me noticing people being interested in talking to me, then me talking to them. After one such experience, however, I realized that living by signs is no way to live.

I was sitting at a lounge with a friend having a Tanq and tonic after work. I glanced around for a quick people watch. The place was full of young professionals dressed to impress. A few of them I recognized, but today I was in the mood to meet new people.

There were many who caught my attention. I am open to meeting anyone but sometimes women stand out a bit more than men. The place was full of beautiful, elegant and maybe even interesting young women. I could not help but notice one in particular because she stood out. I saw her sitting three tables away in a bright pink dress. Most of the other people were wearing black cocktail. She was having dinner with a girlfriend just sitting there looking gorgeous.

My feelings screamed out to go talk to her, but the slow rational in me said to calculate the success first. What would her reaction to me be? Did she want to see me?

The rational brain is protective. It is what has kept us from being eaten by saber-tooth tigers all these centuries. It ensures we don't do anything too crazy. *Any base jump higher than 10 feet needs to be accompanied by a parachute or bungee cord,* says the rational brain. Where would we be without the safe calculations?

The rational brain starts asking its questions. *What is the probability that she will be nice and not chew me out like that tiger?* Will she crush my ego, since apparently that needs "protecting" too?

So I do what the rational mind says to do. I calculate. I look for a sign.

*Is she single?*

*Well, it is Valentine's Day and she is sitting with a girlfriend. Chance of single 80%.*

Then, another calculation arises. *Is she interested?*

I get up to grab another drink from the bar. I can't help but notice that as I walk by her table, she glances up at me for half a second while talking to her friend. She notices me.

Now my rational mind says there's a 70% chance she'll be receptive if I talk to her. I would prefer the success odds of sanitizing gel, like 99.99%, but that is like expecting her to walk over and hand me her phone number on a napkin. In the world of 2019, that is not going to happen.

I decide I have enough evidence, so I walk over, say something nice and introduce myself. I don't know what will happen. I just want to meet her.

I read the signs correctly. She thought I was nice. She invited me to help her and her friend help finish their charcuterie board. We exchanged numbers and over a couple of days we texted a few times trying to meet up. After two or three attempts we eventually managed to decide on a time and place.

This was the realization. I did not just need signs to ask her out. I continued to need signs as I communicated with her and went out with her. I did not stop looking for signs at the restaurant. That was just the beginning. Over the next few weeks, with every text message I wondered if she still wanted to go out or if she had lost interest. When we went on a date I wondered if we would be compatible. I wondered if she would enjoy doing the things I enjoyed doing and if we would have things in common. I *continued* to look for signs. I always kept seeking proof that it was going to work out.

After we went out the first time, I still wanted evidence before asking her out again. I'm sure that if we did get into a relationship, I would probably still look for signs. I would wake up every morning wondering if she loved me or cared about me. Why? Because I was a man who lived by signs.

The life of signs is hesitant. If you see the signs you might take action. If you do not you are definitely not putting yourself out there. *She hasn't texted me back, why should I call?* For the man of signs, every action must be queued up by evidence of success.

I am only human after all, it is not my fault. Humanity has always lived by signs. Some of my favorite stories of signs come from the Bible.

Adam and Eve are strolling in the garden, they see the tree. They know the fruit is bad because God said it was. However, it does not give any signs of being bad. "The woman saw that the tree was good for food, and that it was a delight to the eyes," (Gn 3:6); so they disobey what they know from God and follow the signs. They eat the fruit, which seems to be good. Then, they lose paradise. In that case, following a sign was a bad idea.

Great people after Adam and Eve throughout the Bible continued to desire signs.

The story of Moses recounted in the book of Exodus is another example. At the time, God's Chosen People, the Hebrews, were in bondage in Egypt. God tells Moses to go to the Pharaoh and bring back the Chosen People; literally like just go pick up six million people in a rideshare or something and bring them back two hundred and fifty miles to the promised land.

It is often hard for me just to get myself to drive to the gym after work. God's request to rescue the Hebrews from one of the most powerful armies in the world and trek them across a desert seems like a fantasy. The story went something like this.

Moses asks God, "I'm a poor speaker why would the Pharaoh listen to me?" Most of us have said something like that about ourselves, "I'm shy, awkward or short so I can't talk to people."

God, however, gives Moses the power to turn his staff into a snake, which was supposed to impress the Pharaoh. With this staff in his hand Moses feels confident and agrees to approach the Pharaoh.

Only now, after having a sign, was Moses was ready to take action and start his journey.

We all want signs of success before attempting to succeed. Sometimes God gives them. Occasionally, the universe gives in to our request and drops a flare. We all want to hold that magical staff in our hand, like Moses, before walking into a crowded room to talk to people. If we had that golden staff, yes, we would talk to everyone. Without it, though, we hold back. The sign does not make us different people though, it just gives us permission to take action, permission which we never really had to ask in the first place.

We always want God to shower signs that, whatever the case, everything is going to work out. Great men have sought signs and lesser men have also needed them. It is part of the human condition.

Moses was one of the greatest of the biblical leaders and even he felt the need for some sort of visible evidence that his approach to the Egyptians would not end in absolute rejection.

God turned his staff into a snake. And then God the snake turned it back into a staff. OK, that would do.

## The sign way

Nowhere are signs still as sought out as in our social encounters. Introverts love signs. Naturally inclined to analyze and judge, the powerhouse introvert mind will break down every sign and tell you what it means.

He will reread a text message a dozen times before deciding what the appropriate response will be.

The introvert will stay up till midnight wondering what the words, "Nice to meet you," actually meant from a midday conversation. *Was he just being nice? Or does he want to see me again?*

People would kill for a sign in romance, some indication that the person they like likes them back. A man rarely walks up to that girl at a wine bar and talks to her unless he has some indication that she will be receptive. A girl is more likely to invite that guy over to her table if he can manage to make eye contact with her for at least two seconds. The heart wants what it wants, but the mind wants signs first.

Romance is not the only place we look for signs. Something similar happens in other social situations as well. The college grad sees the circle of Armani-suited business professionals at a networking event. Does he break in and introduce himself? Or does he wait for someone to notice him and invite him over?

We were not born that way. We were born to go after what we want. If a baby wants milk she asks for it. If a child sees Winnie the Pooh at the theme park he goes and gives him a hug.

I've seen my own seven-year-old niece talk to people. She couldn't care less if the girl in front of us at the grocery checkout said hello or not. If my niece thinks the child's *My Little Kitty* earrings are cute she will tell her so. She does not need signs. I'm not sure if she knows signs even exist.

At some point in time, we began seeking approval before engaging in interactions with other people. We decided we needed signs before we could be social. We alienated ourselves from what we wanted and started living by what society apparently wants from us. We began perceiving the world as a dangerous place and self-preservation of the ego became the priority. If we only knew, however, that the ego is really the only thing standing between us and what we want.

The Gospel message on signs is two sided. On one hand, it recognizes that we seek signs. The Old and New Testaments tell stories of good people who want proof that they will succeed before they try. On the other hand, it says we need to grow out of it if we want great things to happen.

This makes me think, what do you do when you receive no signs? Do you just become powerless?

What do you do when you walk into the networking room ready to meet people but no one so much as glances at you? You walk to the bar to grab a drink, still no signs. So you retreat to the corner and huddle your vodka Sprite to your chest and pull out your phone as if you had something important to do.

What do you do when you speak to someone for 30 minutes but receive no indication that they would like to see you again?

What do you do when you see someone you like but you have not been on a date in five months and you are wondering if you are even datable? Where is the sign that you are good enough?

If you are habituated to acting by signs are you capable of acting without them?

Sometimes in life there are no signs, but the social man must still act.

Also, sometimes you read the signs incorrectly. You thought someone wanted to meet you but they were just smiling at the person behind you. There is no way to be right 100% of the time with the signs. It would take a social genius to read them all correctly and act appropriately.

## Something better than signs

Signs are good and they can be helpful in life. Signs help you make it across the street without being run over by a car. You need to be able to read the signs to get through life. And that is OK, if all you want to do is just get through life.

The journey of 72 books of the Bible was to create another type of man, a superior man. This person can read the signs but he is also *independent* of the signs. Social interactions are one area of life where you can completely ignore the signs and talk to whomever you want. I give you permission. God gives you permission.

**Faith needs no permission to take action. It may not know what the outcome will be but it does not care.**

This superior person lives by Faith. The life of signs is a life of reaction to other people's actions. The superior being is a visionary, not a reactionary. He can see what he wants before it happens. His vision *makes it happen.* He sees someone and already envisions himself having a great time talking to that person.

This is Faith. It is the direct approach. Faith needs no permission to take action. It may not know what the outcome will be but it does not care. It simply seems like the right thing to do. So Faith does it.

Many good people, Moses included, live by signs. The superior being is called to be even greater than Moses and live by Faith.

You believe someone wants to see you again so you send them an invite.

The sensitive introvert may think himself clever for knowing how to read the signs. He becomes very good at it to the point of knowing if the person he passed in the hall would like to meet him or if the one standing next to him in the elevator would like to say hi. Really, though, what is the point? Pursuing what you want by Faith will always be the superior path.

## No time to read

I realized at one point that I do not have time to live by signs. Life is short and youth is passing. I don't have six decades to learn to read all the signs of life. I do not have time to master the art of reading body language or listen between the lines. I do not want to live reacting to things I see. I want to act now. I want to act creating what I want.

Signs are "safe", they keep us from getting hurt; they minimize the risk. They keep us on a road where everybody else is going, getting the results that everybody else seems to get. You only see what everyone else sees. You never have your own vision. However, I have started to see that to get to where you are called to go you need to see what no one else sees. Only belief can do that.

The capable man sees a sign and can respond to it. The superior man is that and more. He does not despise signs. He acknowledges them; he enjoys them; gives thanks to God for them. He is encouraged by them, but he is fully capable at any moment and in any place of believing and acting without them and when God puts someone in his path, he does not need signs to say hello.

If there is something he really wants, he will even go off-road and act against the signs. You see that person locked in their world of ear buds and phone screen. You have no indication that they would like to talk to you. It appears they want to be left alone, but you go over and say hello anyway and it ends in you making a new friend.

God's entire relationship with man from Adam to you has been a journey of getting man to live by Faith rather than by signs.

Man wants signs that God is still there so God sends them.

Man wants signs that God loves him so God feeds five thousand people with five loaves and two fish (Mt 14:13-21). Only love can do that.

What God really, wants, however, is for the man to become superior and work without signs. This is the man who will overcome the fear of rejection.

A man can grow from the signs God gives him and build Faith. Or he can become weaker and more dependent on signs. He eventually wants more miracles, more money, more promotions, and more friends before he will start to believe in himself or God.

The man of Faith decides that God is going to be his friend before he sees the signs. He decides God likes him because he knows he's likable and he can't find a serious reason for God not to like him. He does not walk into church wondering if God wants him there. If God created him, why wouldn't God love him?

I began to see people the same way. Unless someone is wearing an "I Hate John" shirt, I know they will love me.

Faith is the superior way to build a relationship. The man of Faith pursues God because God is good, not because God has given evidence of prosperity or good things to come. Faith is also the superior way we relate to each other.

He decides he is going to make a relationship happen. He puts one foot in front of the other, he walks straight to church, he kneels, and he begins to speak. No signs given. No cares given. It is just Faith.

In this journey, I realized that the Faith that stands between God and me matters. It is the same Faith that connects me with other people. It also connects me with myself. If I seek signs from God, I will also seek signs from people. I am waiting for evidence that they like me before I reach out to encounter them.

If I seek signs from God, I will also seek signs from myself. Every day is a constant search for proof that I am "good enough". Only then can I be happy with myself.

The man of signs is different from the social man. Someone attractive swipes right on the man and his mood goes up.

Then his date flakes on him and the mood goes down.

The girl he asked out at the coffee shop texts him back. Mood is up again.

The networking happy hour he attended was a bust and the mood is back down again.

One week he had between eight and ten positive interactions with people so it was a good week.

The next week he spends every evening studying for a certification exam so life goes back to lame.

When signs are present, your courage is in a bull market. Eventually, the market crashes though. And when it does,

**You can say hi in the park**

your shoulders slump and you are staring down at the floor or at your phone looking for memes to distract you from your boredom. That is no way to live.

Some people refuse to do anything until they get a sign. If none of the good signs are present, if we had a week of sad signs or no signs then we clam up, we stay in and feed our emotions on the streaming network of fake drama. That is the life of signs.

The biggest lie of the social contract is that we need the approval of others before we can take action. You probably signed that contract sometime in middle school when you became hyper self-conscious around others, but now it is time to break it.

The life of Faith comes before results not after. You believe, you envision and then it happens. Why? Because it is precisely the belief that makes things happen. Jesus Christ had three years of public life to spend with us. He spent all three of them trying to teach that lesson.

Believe. Behave as if it were going to happen. Live as if it already were happening.

God used centuries of Old Testament stories trying to convince the Chosen People that. Believe first. Abraham, Moses, Joshua, and the story of Gideon outnumbered nearly five to one against the Midianite army. It is belief that *makes* victory happen. Enjoy the signs of success, but stop needing them in order to succeed.

The journey of Faith is not the easy path, but it is the path of adventure. It is all the thrill of the blind date with none of the disappointment because Faith never fails. The act itself is the reward.

Faith requires daily work, time alone, intentional meditation, an act of will, and certainly a mentor or friend to slap you out of your sign-driven lifestyle from time to time.

However, I do not yet know of any alternatives. Jesus did not say, "One way to move a mountain is to have Faith." There is only one way to move the mountain and that is with Faith.

I wanted to move a mountain once. I wanted to change when change seemed impossible. I was quiet and shy. I wanted to be able to meet new people anytime, anywhere. I wanted to become socially comfortable and not have to leave every party after ten minutes.

That seemed impossible, but then I started believing that people wanted to meet me. I started believing that God wanted me to meet them. I started believing that we would have a lot of fun getting to know each other.

There are way more opportunities in the world than there are signs pointing to them. The social man has to believe to access them. He does not wait for people to notice him and give him permission to talk to them. Everywhere he goes he believes he is wanted.

The man can continue interacting with people by signs and continue getting mediocre results or he can act as if they all want to meet him and see some amazing results. The way of signs is obedience to the world. Faith is living by God's plan for you and all the people He has planned for you to meet.

Here is thought number four for the social introvert: *I live by Faith not by signs. I do not need permission to meet people. I believe they want to meet me.* Every time he enters a room, he not only thinks this to be true but *behaves* as if it were true. He shows up in front of everyone like the long-lost friend who is coming to say hello.

# 6

# You are Invited to My Party

*A real conversation always contains an invitation. You are inviting another person to reveal himself or herself to you, to tell you who they are.*

—David Whyte, English poet

## *That was unexpected*

"Are you in line?" she asked.

I was standing inside the doorway of my favorite coffee shop. I would have liked to have been in line, but I was still deciding if I would like a five dollar latte or two dollar coffee.

I turned around and saw the voice behind me. She was cute, 5'6, Disney eyes, with a smart pixie cut and toned arms that said, "I do cross-fit."

"How are you doing?" I returned, feeling a special awesomeness.

"I'm ... good," she returned with some thought. "And yourself?"

"Fantastic, and, no, I'm not in line, you can go right ahead."

"Why fantastic?" she returned.

"Ah, great things are happening today," I responded, which probably meant I had just finished grading a set of quizzes from my Italian 101 class and now had the rest of the day off.

"*Hello. Excuse me, Miss. Take your order?*" The barista stared at us.

She ordered. I ordered. Then it all ended for the moment and we started behaving like normal people staring at our laptops for the next half hour at opposite ends of the coffee shop.

At one point I glanced up and noticed her seat empty. She must have left.

Then, five minutes later, something unexpected happened. I saw a pair of jeans standing behind my Macbook screen. My eyes followed them up and there was Disney Eyes.

"Hi. Uh ... so you wanna like go ride bikes or something later?" she asked. I later learned she had walked to her car, had that *what if* thought and decided to come back into the coffee shop to invite me out.

I immediately said yes while trying to remember if there was a working bike I could borrow from my parents' garage. Yes, by the way, I was living at home and enjoying every moment of it. Later that day, we took our road bikes out on a local trail and I made a new friend.

Meeting new people is great, but if you never invite them out you will probably never see them again. Most of us come across people we want to see again.

The more people we ask or invite the more people will accompany us. Ask less and you will probably spend more of your life alone. Alone time can be heavenly, but admit it; doing cool stuff with cool people is pretty awesome also.

For the social person, it is not enough to have a great world-view, feel great about ourselves, and say hi to people. We must invite, love the invitation, and not care about what the answer will be.

For a long time I have heard people telling me complex existential reasons for why they aren't getting what they want in life, especially in their social life or relationships.

*God is testing me to see if I really love him more than a relationship before I can get into a relationship, so that I will be in a relationship for the right reason.*

*My soul is walking through a desert of consolations so it can be strengthened in preparation for something great coming my way.*

*The right person will come at the right time when I'm ready for her. Then I won't be alone anymore.*

*I'm not good enough, I am not cute enough, I do not make enough money, my generation is married, I'm neither Gen-X nor Gen-Y so I don't fit in. I'll never find someone, or make friends and will be alone forever* ... and so forth.

For a long time I thought it was true. Being social today is challenging. Yes, statistically speaking my generation is married with three kids so it is logical that they would be in a different moment of the life cycle.

Then I made a huge breakthrough and discovered the art of the invitation. It is simple but life changing. If you invite more people to spend time with you more people will spend time with you.

The science is simple and it is even in the Bible. "Ask and it will be given to you" (Mt 7:7). Yes, and even sometimes ask the same person more than once.

At some of my talks I have polled audiences of young professionals and emerging adults. I have asked the men how often they ask someone out.

They respond, "Once every two or three months." It is not a surprise that people complain about their dating lives. From the people I have spoken to, however, I think something similar happens in friendships or even professional connections. How often do you personally invite people to spend time with you?

"Hey, I am having a party. Come join." Every invitation is an invitation to a party because everything you do is a celebration. That is how the social person lives life.

God also thinks we do not ask enough. He reminds us that most of us quit too soon and do not ask enough.

*Ask and you shall receive, knock and the door will be opened* (Mt 7:7). Ask over and over again. I not only have to ask, I have to ask frequently.

*Because of his persistence he will rise and give to him* (Lk 11:5). Eventually, you get what you ask for.

The theme of asking is very strong in Christian culture. God encourages us to ask him without shame or embarrassment. God Himself sets the example by asking of us without hesitation,

"Come follow me." (Mt 4:19)

"Come and see." (Jn 1:39)

It is easy to invite people, but there is also a very real reason why many of us do not invite people. It is the almighty feeling of rejection. If you ask someone they might say no. Who wants to go through that? No, in any shape or form, could ruin your day. It fills your gut with bad thoughts and you start thinking bad thoughts like, "Am I good enough," or "Is there something wrong with me?"

In my journey I went from somebody who never invited people out to someone who invites people weekly. I still prefer a yes over a no, but rejection is not something I think about anymore. These are the lessons that got me there.

\*\*\*

## Rejection is my spirituality

I once used to think about the "no's" I got in life. I worried less about it when I realized people say no to God all the time. They even nailed his Son to a cross. If people said no to Jesus Christ, most likely the most social man in human history who was simply perfect, they will definitely say no to me. That is to be expected.

Seek the no. Stop avoiding it. Good Friday is the ultimate rejection day for Christians. It is the day that mankind rejected the Son of God and killed him.

One year, I had the day off on Good Friday. I decided I would use the day to get rejected as much as possible. I started off by going for a little exercise. As I was out for my jog and running errands I decided to talk to everyone I felt like talking to. I wanted to feel rejection, the same rejection that Christ felt. I wanted people to tell me, "Get lost," or just turn away and ignore me. I talked to people on the bike path, at the coffee shop, at the grocery store. Unfortunately, no one rejected me or told me to disappear. Everyone was pretty friendly or even flattered that I went out of my way to talk to them. I learned that the very possibility of rejection is what makes good things happen.

Inviting people is not even about "getting a date" or being surrounded by friends on a night out. It is about the type of person you want to be. I had to ask myself, "Do I want to be the type of person who invites people to join his life? Do I want to be an inviter? Somebody who shares his life with others? Or do I want to be someone who stands by helplessly watching opportunities float on by and keeps to himself?" Asking actually has little to do with hoping to spend time with people and more to do with the type of person you want to become.

Some people want to learn to invite better for romantic reasons. Occasionally, men have asked me, "How do you just go up to people and talk to them?" Again, asking is not about trying to get into a relationship. Even people who are already in a relationship need to ask.

I once heard a married guy say he was too scared to ask his wife if he could take an evening off to go out with the guys. "She won't like that," he said in a timid voice. I thought to myself, *They are married, they aren't supposed to be afraid of each other anymore.* I wonder, though, if people who were unafraid of asking while single will be less afraid of asking while married.

Either way, asking in romance is always hard, especially for men. As a fundraiser, I once thought that asking people for money was the hardest thing ever. Then I started asking people out and suddenly I developed a stutter, a slur, and began experiencing mind blackouts. Really, I think a lot of men would rather ask a woman to be their kidney donor than to be their date.

In Scripture, there is a good way and a not so good way to ask. Don't ask with hesitation. Do ask decisively, absolutely convinced that this is what you want and this is what you will get. Some people call that arrogance, but really it is just Gospel.

"All things you ask, ask in prayer, believing, you will receive." (Mt 21:22)

Being decisive in your ask will often determine whether or not you will get what you are asking for. God wants you to be decisive when you ask him. People also want you to be sure of yourself or at least sure of your actions when you approach them for something. Nobody wants to give to someone who is unsure of what he wants.

In my Christian spirituality asking should never be timid, neurotic, or shy. It is bold and definitive. "I tell you, whatever you ask for in prayer, believe that you have received it, and it will be yours" (Mk 11:24).

Other times Christ was so confident he did not even ask. He just told people, "Come follow me" (Mt 4:19).

I don't think Jesus Christ ever said to anyone, "So ... maybe ... if you're up to it, like later we could hang out or something ... or not. Like break some bread together? I dunno, what do you think?" He was very specific, come follow me *right now*.

Confidence in prayer is interesting because, in Christian thought, the way we treat God is often the same way we should treat others. If you ask God with confidence, you are more likely to ask your neighbor, as well, with confidence.

We ask our neighbors for the opportunity to give them something because we are already "like gods". Each of us has countless gifts to give each other: a laugh, good advice, deep friendship, or maybe just a hand to hold. Everything about you is a gift.

**Life is a party. Invite people to join**

Just give me a chance and I will give you a great time. Maybe I will give you an adventure. Whether asking to receive or asking to give it is always with supreme confidence.

People who can comfortably ask God will probably ask people more easily as well. I do not consider myself an exemplary religious person. However, I have dabbled in it enough to notice that people who love God can more easily love the stranger as God's creation.

It is never really the creature we are displeased with, it is the Creator. Everything tastes bitter when it is prepared by someone we do not like. Love the Creator and it is easier to love the creation.

Develop a good relationship with the Creator and everything else will start to fall into place more easily. Your relationship with society changes. There are no more "strangers" for everyone belongs to the same creation. There aren't two groups of people: those I know and those I don't. We are all part of the same family.

Learn to ask that Creator. He never says no. He might take forever. It may not happen even in this life; but he never says no. Eventually, everybody gets what they want, according to the Christian promise.

I like to ask small.

I first ask for a happy morning or a peaceful evening.

I ask him to put inspiring people in my path.

I ask for the opportunity to make somebody's day.

I ask for peace in my heart and emotions.

God knows what you want before you even ask. That certainly makes it easier to ask.

## Nobody knows what you are thinking

People are different. People generally don't know what you are thinking about. I could be thinking about rock climbing, sex, tacos, or God and the person behind me in line at the grocery store will not have a clue. I have to be honest, direct and express my intentions if I want people to know them. I have to invite people if I want to spend time with them.

Society has no idea what you need or want. Apart from your mom and Jesus Christ, few people in life are going to give you what you want without asking.

Asking needs to become as common and easy as ordering dinner off a phone app. At first you don't want the food to go to the wrong place. You want to make sure there's extra tzatziki sauce, so you overthink it, check and double-check and analyze it to death. You make sure the apartment number is correct. No sense in sending Allen downstairs a bag of gyros.

With time, however, ordering becomes easy and thoughtless. You press on your phone a few times while in a corporate meeting, barely thinking about it; a short while later lunch is at your office desk . When you can do it without really thinking about it, then you can really do it.

"Ask and you shall receive," (Mt 7:7) Jesus's call to all people to ask more.

Sometimes people worry about asking too much or appearing needy. They try things like wait three days, never invite more than once a week, go off grid for three months and then get back in touch. Nobody wants to appear needy or too available. A simple solution is to not be needy then you will not appear needy.

Like everything else, neediness begins in the thoughts. If you think you are needy, then you are needy. Inviting people less will not make you less needy. So how often should you ask? There is no limit.

Ask as often as you like. Sometimes I've invited people every single day of the week to do something with me because I felt like spending time and sharing experiences with people. There is nothing more genuine than a feeling. If you feel like having people around you, invite them out. If you feel like connecting with someone, reach out.

Let's put it this way. If I didn't have a job and saw ads for jobs I wanted I would probably ask for one three or four times a week and upload my resume to every HR department that had a job I was at least minimally interested in.

You may only get about a tenth of what you ask for in life so asking continually is important. Eventually, it becomes a lifestyle. Invite, ask, join me...

Christ walked around Israel basically asking and inviting people to hang out, some for an afternoon on a hillside eating bread and fish, others he invited to accompany him for the rest of his life. He invited them to share in his purpose.

Thousands accompanied him and many also said, "No thanks." Sometimes the most unexpected people said yes, like the Roman centurion. Other times those who should have said yes, his own people, ignored him.

There are no rules on who you can talk to, who you can invite, or how often you can invite.

I remember thinking once that I was not supposed to talk to people at the gym. You just put your lifting face on, pretend you don't see anybody, and start moving weights.

*People are working out. You can't talk to them, man.*

Then I started saying hi to people I felt like saying hi to. Some barely said hello back, others went out to lunch with me and a few are regular workout friends and we high five when I walk in the gym and cheer each other on for showing up.

Then I once thought you couldn't go to the bar alone.

I remember riding my bike home from work one day on Main St. and hearing some Spanish guitar playing at one of the bars. I stopped in to listen. A lovely woman at one of the high tables waved me over. I went over.

I told her she was beautiful and introduced myself to her. There was a violin-guitar duo playing so I put in a request for *Por Una Cabeza* and dragged her onto the dance floor for a spot of tango.

I also hit it off with her date, great guy. We exchanged info and he told me to come to his penthouse office kick-off party a month away.

After that I still thought you couldn't talk to people on the bus. Public transportation is like the epicenter of our nation's individuality. You just don't talk to people on mass transit.

So I started talking to people on the bus to see what would happen. They were mostly medical professionals going to work like myself.

There was one I thought was really cute, Amanda the dietician. I decided to be honest with her and asked her out. She had a boyfriend, but she was happy I invited her out. I felt good and I realized that the result of the invitation never really matters; it is about the experience.

People talk about being afraid of inviting people to spend time with them. Nobody is really afraid of asking questions. It is the answer we fear. If we knew people would always say yes to us we would ask all the time. The possibility of "no" makes us anxious. And this is how the introvert overcomes the rejection or the no. Stop thinking about the answer. Just enjoy asking the question. Bathe in that experience and give thanks you had the opportunity to invite somebody.

Or perhaps, imagine a life in which people tell us yes so often that we care little for the few no's we get.

## Rejection dies with a thought

Some people think you just have to get used to rejection. After a while you are desensitized and stop caring. It is like developing a rough hand.

The first time you do a set of pull-ups on a cross-fit bar the skin on your hands rips. Eventually, however, you build callouses and your hands become rough and tough.

You ask people. People say no. You are hurt at first, but you get tough and used to it. This happens after dozens, if not hundreds, of occurrences though. How long will it take? I don't know, maybe a few years.

Imagine, though, if you could skip all that and begin asking people tomorrow without feeling any pain of rejection. You do not need to spend months or years callousing your hands.

What if the fear of rejection that holds you back could disappear tomorrow? What if you could find a way to be so full that no one could take any feeling away from you by saying no?

Does such a way exist? I believe so. I know so because I know I do not have years to get over rejection. I just have today. If I'm lucky and God gives it to me, I have tomorrow also; but there are no guarantees.

I change the way I think about inviting people and seven seconds later inviting people becomes easier. Rejection lives in the mind and only the mind can overcome it. Fortunately, I can change my thoughts in less time than it takes to check my social media notifications.

During that spontaneous bike ride with the girl from the coffee shop years ago, I got a chance to learn a lot about her and her life. She had a great personality and her life was full of friends, a meaningful career, and family. She didn't need me to say yes. She did not need me to go bike riding with her. She would have been fine alone. She was just curious about me and was inviting me to share an experience with her.

As I write this I'm texting Franky, the carefree downtown trial lawyer I met at the bar last week.

*Wanna grab drinks after work?*

He may say yes or he may say no. But it doesn't matter. Whatever the outcome, I have this thought in my mind: *No one can reject me because I am not asking for anything. I only invite others to share what I have. My party is open. You are invited.*

# 7

# Too Many Knights on the Field

*If you want to achieve great deeds, exert yourself,*
*take up arms, fight as you should, go everywhere across*
*both land and sea...*

—Geoffroi of Charny, The Book of Chivalry

## Let me get that for you

I was at the brewery sipping on a lemon water while my friends hammer-fisted heavy glasses of stout. I do not drink beer. From close to my elbow a cute voice called out, "So will someone buy me a drink or is chivalry dead?"

I looked over at her and wanted to buy her a drink so badly. Dang, this was my chance to be chivalrous. My instinct told me, *Do it! Rise up to the occasion. Be a real man. Show the world that chivalry is not dead and there are still good men out there. Put her on your water tab.*

And then I thought, *Is that a good reason to do that? To be liked? To prove something?*

Reasons aside, the incident made me think. *How should a real man behave in society? What does a real man do? Does he buy drinks for every woman in arm's reach? Is his priority to please people?*

Are we supposed to be warm and fuzzy like the Starbucks barista or casually wink at the sidewalk paparazzi like the movie star walking into the bistro for Saturday lunch?

Are we supposed to be nice? But not too nice? Are there certain behaviors that are specifically proper for a man? The cheetah runs, the bear can claw, but what about the man? How does he behave?

It is hard to have a discussion on male behavior without recognizing the impact of the modern chivalry movement, a fairly widespread movement to reform male behavior in society. The movement tells men today that chivalry is their ticket to social respectability and even love.

The message is simple: *Be nice and you will be respected, a nobleman.*

Early in my professional life, I was searching for ways to rebuild my social network after moving to a new city for the tenth time. In an effort to be a better man in society, I took a small sip of the chivalry lemonade. I decided: I'll try some of these things they are talking about.

Everybody and their cat want men to be more chivalrous. If only men would open more car doors, pick up the tab and be nicer society would be a better place. If men could be more chivalrous people could enjoy dating again also. The workplace would be less toxic. The whole world wants a world of nice men.

For a split second it seemed they were selling some good stuff. Be nicer and more people will like you. Is that the essence of manhood? Be nice in order to fit in?

I soon realized, though, that this was more of a playful thought than actual reality. This modern chivalry was a fun game of Legos, but to build a real high-rise you need a deeper foundation than just polite behavior. The core of social strength needs to be something more than this.

Any man who has tried to do these nice things with the intention of connecting better with people knows that at best they will say you are a nice guy. Yep, you become a nice guy; that is it. That is the essential outcome of the modern chivalry movement.

## *Too many knights on the field*

That is also why chivalry, as many people understand it, is not working. It is based on the principle, "Be nice and society will accept and appreciate you." The whole intention of the chivalry movement is to avoid rejection. It does not create a man who can face rejection. It creates one who fears social rejection more than ever but modifies his behavior hoping to minimize it. Modern chivalry produces a man whose ultimate goal is to be accepted by society; and that is the opposite of the social man.

Deep connection does not happen by *doing* things. It is too easy to just do. No one will offer you respect or much less love you simply because you brought flowers. It is a nice thought that a few simple techniques could change all our relationships. But think about it. Who wants to be friends with someone who does nice things just to make friends?

Early on in my life, I, too, tried to be nice to make friends. Then I realized my first lesson in manhood and chivalry. If you are being nice to please people you may as well let a zombie scratch your neck and walk around dead for the rest of your life. There is no soul in a people pleaser for his actions do not come from within. They are controlled by the circumstances. He belongs to society but not to himself. The social man, however, is who he is independent of society.

Imagine if chivalry were really about opening doors or walking between a girl and the street.

Creepy ice cream truck serial killers also open doors for people so how can door opening separate the chivalrous man from the non-chivalrous man?

Chivalry is buying a drink for someone. A lonely man with lots of money will also be happy to buy drinks for young ladies. Surely that cannot be chivalry?

## The first knight

The same actions done by two very different people carry a very different meaning. Chivalry has to be much more than a list of actions. It must be something deeper. I started to read about the origins of chivalry. What made this mounted warrior such an esteemed member of society? Why has contemporary society decided to refurbish superficial bits and pieces of this ideal?

The word chivalry comes from the French *chevalier*, which means horseman. The knight was a mounted badass. The knight had a horse and the horse was the ability to fight an enemy in a superior manner. The knight was a man of superior confidence that probably bordered on arrogance. Sitting on his horse, he rose above the average fighter. He was at the top of the pyramid in the art of war.

The *Book of Chivalry* was a treatise on the essential qualities of the knight, written by a knight himself, Geoffroi of Charny.

The knight was a warrior. "Deeds of arms in war are the most honorable," the 14th century book states. He had to go to war. There was simply no way you could be an honorable knight if you didn't take up the fight.

You can tilt your helm to every damsel in the country, you can pick up checks for your posse until your account bounces, but if you are unwilling to go to war it values as nothing. Chivalry dies when men begin trying to please the world rather than fighting to make a change in it.

I, too, began to see the real moments when chivalry died in me.

I forgot my purpose and mission in the world. I pursued pleasure.

I retreated into the safety of my castle and turned on the TV. It is then that chivalry dies.

Geoffroi also describes one situation in which a knight may become disreputable and undeserving of a woman, or society for that matter:

When the knight has lost his purpose and becomes a "miserable wretch who, for no good reason, is unwilling to bear arms (20, 15)." The fight is everything. A knight who is not fighting for something is just a pile of steel.

When he no longer goes to war, when he stays at home and lives in comfort, he is then nothing to be proud of. It is not manners that make the knight; it is this purposeful sense of fight.

"This love can be worth nothing, nor can it last for long without the ladies wanting to have no more of it and withdrawing (20, 30)." Geoffroi predicts that a man who has given up on his purpose, who has abandoned the war, will also lose the esteem of women.

It is not the man who does nice things who embodies chivalry. It is the man with a driven purpose and mission. He has fun and enjoys life, but at the end of the day, that mission holds priority over his schedule. His use of time and resources are all focused on preparing and engaging him for the fight.

The greatest challenge to chivalry was comfort and laziness. Geoffroi repeatedly says that excess comfort is the man's greatest enemy. When he ceases to go to battle and focuses his efforts on feeling good, living in luxury, then he ceases to be a real man. He dishonors chivalry when he is more concerned with appearing fashionable than with fulfilling his life mission.

The knight was a man of risk. When knights were not fighting in war, they were competing in tournaments during which it was not uncommon to lose a finger, a hand or even life itself. Then, when the knight did go to war, he put everything at risk: his fortune, his health, his life.

The knight embraced risk, the fear of failure, the possibility of rejection. He did not spend his life worrying about what society thought of him. His energies were dedicated to something much bigger, the mission, the fight. He lived in real danger.

Risk is more foreign to us today. Most guys are just trying to hold a job and make the annual merit increase. Carrying out some great mission in society with the possibility of failure is something above and beyond their scope.

Even socially, technology has left us so many ways of encountering people without risk. Swipe and forget. "Wave" at someone through an app from a hundred miles away; send a request to connect with the touch of a button. Rejection is mitigated or gone, and along with it the glory of doing integrating craziness and spontaneity into human interactions. That is fine, technology can be a big help; however, if it is our only or principle way of encountering people we are missing out on the glorious experience of risk and rejection.

Chivalry dies when men play it safe, worry about failing, and stop taking chances.

The knight was a man of self-decision. He pursued what he wanted and nothing got in his way. If he wanted to go on

**You can say hi on the street**

a crusade or fight in a foreign land he did so. The fight came first; family and love could not hold him back. He was convinced and confident of his direction. Chivalry dies if men lose their ability to think and decide for themselves.

I remember often sending the "Wanna do something this weekend?" text. It could be a friendly invite showing I am flexible and would like to meet up. Or it could also be a sign that I really have no direction in my employment of time and no idea what I want to do this weekend. The chivalrous man is sure, very sure of what he wants to do.

A battle to fight, confidence in success: without these things, there is no knight. Without these things the warrior becomes a lost vagabond, an errant struggling to "just get by".

He is a mediocre horseman trying to prove himself to the world through lesser deeds but avoiding the great battle he was created to fight. He gives up against his worst enemy: the ego, which holds him hostage because it is too scared to fail or risk rejection.

Take the mission and the war out of chivalry and you are left with the tin shell of a man seeking to win approval by the shine in his armor or the weave of his tweed blazer.

Take the self-decision out of chivalry and you are left with the "Nice Guy" who is agreeable and everyone likes to have around but nobody will make a baby with.

What is your mission? Why are you on this planet? What is the one dream you have when your dream girl is not around?

The man without the mission is Paris from the Trojan story. He uses tricks to steal a woman he never deserved. He cannot keep the woman he steals because he is not strong enough. He is not a warrior. He is a man of pleasure. Then, the true warriors and the Trojan horse come and lays waste to everything and those around him.

He will sacrifice his city to satisfy his lust for comfort. He has no direction in life but self-pleasure. And he loses everything in the pursuit of pleasure. The Greeks destroy his city and he ultimately dies.

In the end, the un-chivalrous man uses life to build a bubble of comfort around himself instead of doing something good for others. The universe comes to collect because life was given to him to build meaning and he has sold it for a single pleasure. The Trojan horse enters when he least expects it. It lays waste, ruining the world around him.

## I'll do anything for you

There may be men today who will do anything for love and approval but have no direction. Finding love becomes their goal in life instead of doing something meaningful for the world. Without direction, can a man really do anything good for a woman? What contribution will he make to society? The essence of the social man is the ability to contribute something positive to the world around him. That is where his sociability comes from. Identify your purpose and connecting with people becomes so much easier. Identify your purpose and you will care less who rejects or ignores you. This man is not social to avoid loneliness. He is social because he has something valuable to give.

Chivalry is good but when it produces a man who does nice things so society will accept him, I think it is more of a disservice to the developing man. He eventually finds himself willing to trade anything—even his life purpose—for love or somebody's approval. In that moment, chivalry dies.

The world is full of men who will do anything for love or companionship. Most women can log into a dating app this afternoon and by evening find a man (of some sorts) who will take her out to dinner and spend the entire evening with her. Being willing to do something for companionship does not differentiate you from everyone else.

Pleasing people is all the rage right now. I know some men like to read "what women like" blogs in an attempt to improve their relationship ability. Adam asked the question "What do women like?" Eve said women liked forbidden fruit so he ate the apple and lost all eternal paradise. Weather you are a man or a woman, giving up your purpose to please others never ends well.

Adam had everything a man could want: the beautiful girl, retirement at 30, free food. He did not need to work another day in his life. He lost it all when he lost sight of what a man should be. The guy had one job, don't eat the forbidden fruit. Instead, he decided to live his life pleasing people.

The lost knight in Geoffroi's book never thinks of what God likes or what men should be like. He forgets why God placed him in this world; he ignores his calling and lives for approval. Rejection is his greatest enemy and the feeling of comfort is his greatest friend.

The modern chivalry movement creates men who will do anything for love. He will show up with a bouquet of roses or make reservations for a *Michelin* style restaurant to win someone over. The social man will do simply everything with love whether he gets love back or not. He will fill his surroundings with love, whether the world appreciates him or not.

## The new chivalry and the social man

"Do to get" men are easy to come by, but fewer are the men who will simply become a man because he loves masculinity. He loves this epic creation of God that is designed to be strong, calm, unwavering, and productive. Manhood is his proud achievement. He lives with a defined purpose to make everybody's lives better, not just the lives of those he may want love from.

This is a more meaningful chivalry, the one where I fulfill the purpose that I have been born with. My first purpose is to be a real man. If holding a door open for someone identifies with that purpose then I do it. If it is consistent with my idea of manhood then I will do it every day for everyone and at every opportunity I get.

We all know what we would like to get from the world, but it is much more difficult to decide what we will give. If I do not have a mission I do not know what I have to offer the world, all I think about is what I am receiving from the world and rejection hurts more than ever. The authentically chivalrous and social man is absolutely focused on his purpose. When that purpose is the most important thing in the world to him, social rejection matters much less.

This is chivalry and the sixth thought of the social man. Before and after meeting people he thinks: *I live in the world with a purpose. That purpose is more important than anything that could happen to me today. It is bigger than rejection. It is bigger even than me.*

# 8

# Adventure is Currency

*I just can't get enough of this beautiful life*

*- The Collection*

## Buy adventures and everything follows

From my earliest days I remember people telling me, "You need to sacrifice, give, invest in your social life and relationships." And for a while I thought it was true. Make a sacrifice for somebody and your bond will strengthen. You have to give if you want to get something back.

Then I had an experience that made me think otherwise.

I was hanging out on Lake Travis, Austin with some friends. I love the water. I love boats. My ideal day is to exist in

**You can say hi on the metro**

sandals and boardshorts floating on the lake. At that moment, I was doing something I really enjoyed doing.

Then an acquaintance I had made a few weeks earlier invited me to her house party an hour away. She seemed really nice, I liked her. I wanted to get to know her more. Leave the lake early to get a chance to spend time with this girl?

*Maybe we'll go out later. She seems cool.*

Sacrifice something to get something else in return?

I made the wrong choice. I went to the house party. I didn't really connect with anyone there, and the girl who invited me was actually distant much of the time.

I still made a good time of it. I cracked some jokes, laughed with people, and then enjoyed a quiet vodka soda on the porch before leaving. However, I also thought in the back of my head, *I could still be at the lake with fishies tickling my feet in the water.*

At that moment I realized that in social relationships and romance you are happier if you never do anything to get something in return. Just do what you enjoy doing.

Just spend time with people because you enjoy them. Go to the patio bar because you love being there. Show up at that networking event because you are curious about what other people do. If I ever have a hard time deciding which one to go to, the only question I need to ask is, "Where will I have a good time?"

Don't hope that something good will come of it. Stop wondering where it will go. Never go anywhere hoping to get something back. Doing to get is called an investment.

An investment is giving in hopes of expecting something in return. If you buy stocks you want bigger stocks back in return. You put your own money in and you want more money back. You are not just doing it out of good will. Then if you do not get something back you are sad. That is how investments work.

That is also the genesis of disappointment: hoping to get something from someone else who has no commitment to you. You can reciprocate giving, you can enjoy it when others reciprocate, but if you expect someone to give you something back you are setting yourself up for sadness.

"I'm going to say hello to that girl. Hopefully, she will go out with me."

"I'm going to dress up tonight. Hopefully, someone will come talk to me."

"I'm going to take her out to a nice restaurant. Hopefully, she will be impressed."

"I'm reserving the executive club at the stadium; hopefully more people will come to my party."

I've even heard: "I'm going to invite those people to my wedding; hopefully they will bring nice gifts." That is not the social ideal I want to live with.

Imagine giving and expecting nothing in return. The social man does not pursue investments. He seeks experiences. Every experience begins with an act of giving, not taking.

This is why walking into a human encounter emotionally empty-handed does not leave you a lot of options. You have nothing to give.

I noticed that when I don't have much to give, I also expect more back. But the morning I wake up feeling like a billionaire I have plenty to give and expect nothing back.

✳✳✳

## Living for the experience

I remember once being on a sailing tour traveling along the Croatian coastline. We came into port on the island of Milna. I was standing on the deck looking out on the bar scene spread out on the dock. The murmurs of evening conversations, a cover musician playing "Stand by Me", the flow of liquid Tiki.

I was leaning against the starboard rail looking out on the scene. A fellow Australian traveler came up beside me to take it all in. He pointed out two beautiful young ladies having a drink at a bar table on the pier.

"Ay mate, you recon those ladies are single?" Single or not I had to know who they were. Beauty is God's gift to the world and to ignore a beautiful gift is a mortal sin. Or something like that.

I immediately walked across the gangplank to go talk to them. They were a little shocked at first but turned out to be friendly, welcoming and engaging. The taller one ordered me a drink I as I conversed with her friend, a petite blonde. She had a 100-word English vocabulary and I could only say thanks in German, but we instantly felt a connection. We talked as much we as we could and then just smiled when we couldn't understand each other. In the moment I fell in love or maybe was just in love with the moment. It did not matter, it was a wonderful experience.

Realistically, I don't know what I was thinking. Somewhere in my rational brain a thought was being put together, *What's the point, man? This girl is visiting Croatia from Austria. You live in Texas. You're probably never going to see her again. What are you getting out of this?* From a relationship perspective this was a "poor" investment.

It is not about what you get out of it though. It is the experience. Maybe we will be together forever. Statistics say we won't, but who cares? I don't want anything back. I just want to enjoy the moment.

Talking to a beautiful woman by the evening Adriatic sea, walking her home and feeling her fingers in your palm; there is value in all that, immense value. That is a gift from God. And that is enough for me.

## Show up to give

The truly social being does not do something to get something back. His reward is already the present moment. He is never anxiously waiting for results. Anxiety is toxic waste for social interaction. If you have anxiety, stay home and take care of it. Then go out.

People speak of other people being toxic. What is toxic is anxiety. It will destroy your social capacity. You never enjoy the present moment because you are thinking of what the end result will be. All the stressed and negative ions leak into your attitude. Instead of simply giving of yourself, you are nervously wondering, *Where is this going? Will my time investment pay off? How will I get her number?*

When you are 5000 miles from home in a country like Croatia it is a little easier to be detached from results. You know you are just passing through.

However, the truth is we are always just passing through. Everywhere we go and at every moment we are passing through. There is no guarantee we will be back or even be breathing tomorrow. All we have is the moment, now, and the people in front of us whether we're standing on a sailing ship or checking avocados in the produce section of our favorite supermarket.

As simple as it sounds I realized there were many instances in my daily routine where I was doing things to get. As I focused to root them out one by one I was finally freed of the Wall Street anxiety that investors go through. I could be truly present and social.

I was no longer an investor. I was a buyer and what I purchased paid off in dividends immediately, not ten years down the road. The whole experience made it worth it. Walking across that gangplank onto the pier was worth it; whether the Tiki bar Austrian smiled, blew me off, came to visit me later in the US or completely forgot me, it was worth it. Whether we shared things in common or not, it was worth it.

Once I could stop doing to get, the freedom became unlimited. Now I could do whatever I wanted independent of the outcome ten minutes or ten seconds from now. Whatever happens doesn't matter. What I do now is all that matters.

The doing to get mentality especially takes all the fun out of dating. You never really enjoy going out with anyone. You are always thinking of a relationship or marriage.

"Do to get" people are boring. *I don't know if I should climb on stage and dance with the lead singer. Will people think I'm weird?* They can't just be themselves.

"Do to get" people are stressed out. *When is he going to text back?*

"Do to get" people are disappointed. *She is "too tired" to go out tonight. Ugh, what a waste of 19 creatively crafted dating app messages.*

"Do to get" people eventually give up. *I've invited eight friends to see this movie with me and no one is available. WTF? What's the point? I'm never inviting anyone out again.*

Is there a place for sacrifice in relationships? I think there is; but it is a sacrifice you enjoy in the moment, you value now. *Sure, I'll go to your party even though I'm tired after work and there's an hour of traffic between us. I'm still going because I want to though. Maybe I won't make a single friend at your party.* That is OK. The social man creates experiences, not results.

Once I stopped expecting anything back from people I could be free to act. I left investing to Wall Street. Now I just buy amazing experiences one at a time.

Thirty years from now, when you start to tell that story, "When I was young..." you will have experiences to tell. Maybe you are single. Maybe you married that Austrian girl you said Hi to at the boat dock bar. Maybe you still have a lot of friends around you, maybe they are gone. It doesn't matter. There is value in the memories. You lived in the moment. You bought adventures and you never regretted it.

Before he decides where he will go out the social man remembers, *The only thing that exists is this moment. I come to society to give, never to take.* I only come to give and to share the amazing present moment with those around me.

## 9

# Put Your Money in Your Mouth

*A man with outward courage dares to die; a man with inner courage dares to live.*

—Lao Tzu, Tao Te Ching

### Where can I meet people?

At one point in my career I quit my job teaching Italian for Purdue University and accepted a position in Houston, Texas, designing medical curriculum. Career wise it was a great move. Socially it was potentially a great move.

I say potentially because I was moving from a city of 70,000 to one of 2.3 million. However, I did not know a single person in Houston. The only person I knew in all of Texas was my new boss. So how do you go from knowing nobody to meeting people?

At the time I believed that the most important thing in meeting people was making the time and the investment.

You need to put money and time into meeting people. Great people are out there, you just need to meet them. Join groups and societies and then more groups.

I was caught in the spiral of thinking I needed to buy more memberships, download more dating apps, "get seen", create more profiles, professional networking, memberships, tickets, vodka tonic, hand shake, side hug and on and on and over and over.

I was single so I even remember clicking on an ad for a matchmaking service to meet more people. You had to dedicate a lot of time and resources specifically to finding people. I thought that's what it took to be social.

My life revolved around trying to meet more people. I didn't have a ton of plans during the week other than social networking or dating.

I went to countless socials sometimes with the sole intention of meeting a cute girl or finding fun new friends. In the moment it was just life, but with hindsight I can see it was such an inferior lifestyle.

All the while I was thinking, *I'm investing in my social life.* But should meeting amazing people be so difficult? Does the pile of sugar need a Super Bowl ad for the ants to come? Do bees need a GPS to find the flowers? Do lions need to go online to find a pride to join? Nature works fine without technology, cellphones and membership dues. Why cannot we?

There gets to be a point when you start to wonder, *Do I really need to spend every evening at events meeting more people or is there something deep inside of me that needs to change? Is it just that I am not being who I was created to be?*

Jesus speaks of salt that has lost its saltiness. It is no longer true to its nature. It no longer is what it was created to be and so now it has a miserable, lonely existence being cast aside

**You can say hi to tall people**

(Mt 5:13). Are we all being true to our nature? When I speak of nature, I mean my nature as a man. Is it possible I have lost some of my manhood?

If a lion is a real lion (has the qualities of a lion) it does not have to try. It just is what it is and life falls into place. It has no trouble finding food or companionship. A real lion catches its prey easily. Other lions want to be in its company.

If things are difficult maybe trying harder is not the answer. I do not believe in trying. I believe in being. Maybe you are better off focusing your efforts on being what you should be.

## People are literally everywhere

Become what you were created to be. A matchmaking service or young professional membership can be fun and introduce you to new people but it generally does not offer deep transformation. I was created to be a man. That means something. My place in society is as a man.

If you are what your authentic nature cries out to be then will people have that much trouble finding you? I realized I don't have to be amazing; I just need to be a real man. Maybe then I could just walk down the street or stand in line for coffee and easily meet people.

If you are what God created you to be then should it not follow that you will be happy?

Let's say I did pay 3k a year to join the all-inclusive young executives' club and meet some cool people. What good would it do me if I am not the person God created me to be? What could I possibly have to offer them?

I began to wonder, *What's holding me back from being the man God created me to be?* That was something to think about.

If I were the man I wanted to be I should have no difficulty connecting with people every single day of the week, effortlessly, without installing six phone apps and draining hours of precious time at events across the city. Nature should do the work for me because God made me to connect with people. He put me on this planet with a purpose and people are part of that purpose.

I would be surrounded with great people. If a bird can always find a nest to rest in then why can't a man find good company to spend life with? If every wolf can find a pack to join why can't every human be surrounded by a supportive community?

Many people suffer from feelings of loneliness. Many of those people also resign themselves to that and never find solutions. I've struggled with the thought. Why would God create a human person just to be alone? That is insane. The first story in the Bible is about a man enjoying the company of another human being, a woman to be specific.

Nobody comes into this world alone, hatching from an abandoned spore. Someone holds them in their hands, their mother, father, the labor and delivery nurse or doula. I have a hard time believing that God then wants those people to live or die alone.

However, I would believe that if the person has not become the type of person God created him to be then, yes, he may be spending a lot of time alone. A bag of coffee that tastes like tea will spend a lot of time on the shelf. I am here with a role or a purpose. It is one I did not choose. But it is still amazing if I will take it up, adopt it, own it. Abandon it and there are no guarantees.

If that man has not embodied what it means to be a real man then, yes, he will be alone. If that woman has not grown the gifts God has given to her then it is possible she will be alone. If the wolf ceased to behave as such and refused to run, would it still be in the pack?

I looked at myself in the mirror and I saw two things: body and behavior. Those are the two things about myself I show the world every single day.

Do I need to change my story?

Get control of my emotions?

Be more positive?

Get healthy?

Be less neurotic? Stop complaining?

What would the ideal man or woman be like?

✳✳✳

## The number one investment

I began to realize that the greatest investment I could ever make would be in myself, not in memberships. You do not need to hold season tickets to the theater or your favorite football team to get someone to spend time with you. You need to give someone something they could never get anywhere else: the real you and your unapologetic purpose. I've been created to do this, come with me.

If you have an empty heart or empty life and no direction then, yes, you will need to spend $300 on Ticketmaster or buy into exciting experiences. If you have a life full of love then you already have a priceless gift.

Most of us do not invest much in ourselves. Maybe we read a book every so often, watch YouTube videos, take a class here and there, or subscribe to a podcast. A serious investment happens, though, by working with a consistent, dedicated, demanding plan that tosses you out of your comfort zone on a daily basis.

I have found that the most challenging and rewarding path to self-improvement is with a personal mentor. Books and learning material can only go so far. The 12 Apostles had scrolls upon scrolls of text describing the coming of the Messiah. They could not make complete sense of it on their own.

They needed to meet the Messiah. They needed to meet the Son of God. They couldn't just read about him. They needed a real person to explain it all and then tell them some things that were never and will never be written as well.

I believe in books but books do not get you out of bed at 5:00 a.m. to start working on your dream. People do. Some of the wisest and most talented people in the world will never write a book. How will you learn what they have to teach if not directly from them? The religion I practice, Catholicism, appreciates books but is more about handing wisdom down through people. We read Scripture but receiving the Eucharist (Christ himself) into you is the ultimate experience.

Nothing is more demanding than working with someone who challenges you where you need it most.

There is a story of Jesus appearing on the shore while the Apostles were fishing in a boat. Peter immediately jumped out of the boat to swim to shore. It was crazy. It was unexpected. It wasn't a book that got him to jump into the water though. It was a person standing on the shore.

When the challenge is great, it is fairly easy to say no to a book. In those moments, however, we generally listen more to people. That is probably why God became man rather than becoming a book. A person can demand of us much more. The challenge is finding the right people to guide us.

The first step to finding a mentor is identifying what you want.

Your goal is you would like to meet more people. Maybe you are too shy and can't get yourself to say hi to anyone.

Find a mentor who helps shy people meet more people. Find someone who has the proven ability to acquire what you want.

Find a specific answer to your specific problem. Often we self-prescribe generic solutions to our challenges.

"I feel depressed, I need a therapist."

"I'm so empty, I need a spiritual director."

While both spiritual directors and counselors have their proper place in healing and self-discovery we fail to dig deeper. If we did, we might realize that what we really feel is bored, powerless, and lonely. We are not achieving what we were created to do.

If there is objectively something wrong with your life you need to identify it and make it better. You may not need a therapist talking to you about new perspectives and the holistic approach. The solution could actually be very simple.

You just need to meet more people and stop spending so much time alone playing with technology. Write your own drama, adventure, or romance. There's a panoramic screen around you every day you step outside your front door.

If you haven't been out with friends in two weeks it is obvious that you will feel lonely. There's nothing wrong with you. It is completely normal. Your social life is on life support, you are not doing anything epic with the rest of your life, so you are sad.

Where does your self-investment ultimately lead you? I once thought it was about "being the one to find the one."

However, it is far simpler than that: *just be who you were created to be.* Forget about the one or the others. If you were created to be a man, be a man. If you were created to be a woman then be a woman. You were made to stamp a mark on this world that no one else can do. Find out what it is.

Fulfilling your created destiny will always be your greatest act of power; and it was never possessions that made you great it was always power. Christ died with only a loincloth around his waist, but he had the power to raise himself from the dead. Power trumps possession. He was God and he had the power of God to show it.

I once asked myself, "How far should I go to become the person I should be? How much time should I dedicate to doing this? Is there a price on it?" There was not one I could think of. So I began putting in the work, whatever it took.

I began to wake up at 5:00 a.m. to do an hour of self-work before going to work. I dipped into my savings to pay a real expert to put me on the right track.

I moved away from family and friends to pursue the career I was called to. Every two years I felt I was leaving something behind but I was gaining so much more. There is no sacrifice too great to fulfill the calling.

A relationship can never replace meaningful self-transformation. The person you were created to be will always cry out from within until you fulfill it or put yourself on the path to fulfilling it.

I don't believe that one person can fulfill another. We are too big for each other. We simply accompany each other on our path to greatness and vocation. If you find the right person, they will accompany you on that journey; but the journey should never be neglected or much less sacrificed to find the person.

If you are who you should be and always show up like a strong man or beautiful woman then dating or friendships just happen. It is important to meet people, but more often than not the investment you need to make is in yourself.

You need to change the way you speak to people. Change where you spend your time. You need to change the way you think about life. Change how you feel, maybe even change how you look. There is no technique to being social, no list of actions to memorize. You just need to change your thoughts and let them carry you.

The transformation and investment bring to light some inconvenient truths. I thought I was a great guy. I had lived as a monk for a decade and a half spending five hours a day in prayer. I had consistently worked every year to uproot bad habits and acquire new ones: change perspectives, learn to love, make sacrifices.

With some introspection I realized a few uncomfortable truths about myself. I was a high functioning machine, always plugged in, but my hard drive had a hidden virus that would make the system crash eventually.

I was lacking several essential qualities of what it meant to be a man. I was reacting to my surroundings, letting the world control my mood, rarely at true peace with myself. My whole life I had formed habits in me that I thought would protect me but in reality, were limiting me.

Worst of all, I had always thought my intentions were pure. However, this hard look at myself taught me I was doing things for the wrong reasons, setting myself up for disappointment.

I changed and started a journey to become a centered, happy man.

I switched from trying to build a great social life to simply building a great life. The two are not exclusive of each other. However, a great life is so much bigger than a relationship or parties.

## *The new life*

My first vocation or calling is not to be married or not married. My first calling is to be a man. "Man and woman he created them" long before he created them to be artists or lawyers. Once I figured that out, I started to feel connected to society in a meaningful way.

It was not easy. I had to do things I was very uncomfortable with. I had to uproot and change long held views of people, the world, and myself. I had to dedicate resources to acquiring knowledge and experience and then putting those to work on a daily basis. For what is learning without action? I dedicated hours each day to daily self-work.

I deleted all the dating apps on my phone. I deleted all the numbers of people I was talking to or going out with. I started over. I was wasting their time until I could find out what it meant to be a man.

Up until then I had traveled the world, lived with a dozen cultures, studied under proficient professors and done things most would only read about in books.

However, I still had an immense amount of transformation ahead of me. I still was not that man. But worst of all, my life had been going in the wrong direction. I was on the verge of settling in so many aspects of my life.

I reset my routine. I stopped going to networking events to meet people. I expanded my oyster to include the whole world. God's children were everywhere: the grocery store, the gas stations, jogging on the streets, the train, the cafeteria.

I identified my worst fears that kept me from being the social man. Every evening after work I spent time conquering those fears. Without fear a man is capable of almost anything. I made it my focus to become the man God had created me to be, in control of his life, breaking down self-created boundaries. I stopped making excuses.

Why can't I ride my bike to a brunch spot on Sunday morning and crash some stranger's family reunion, laugh with them, and ask their daughter out? Who says I can't?

My work improved at my day job. I began to create the happiest moments of my life. I was also further outside my comfort zone than I had ever been. It was not my direct intention, but I went out with more people than I ever had.

I transformed my life. I went from Netflix and chill a couple nights a week to meeting interesting people several times a week, and finding , and writing a book.

I was surrounded by people who gave me life, encouragement, inspiration. Sometimes this was with friends. Sometimes I went out alone finding new friends. Once or twice a week if I made a connection with someone along the way, a date might accompany me.

That starts with being a man or being a woman and all that a man or woman is created to be. Don't worry about being a professor, an engineer, or a geo scientist. First become a man, a real man. Answer the call that is as old as humanity. Become all that it screams out to be but is just too afraid to try. Then the amazing life begins to happen.

Amazing may be painful, it may mean sacrifice. It may be happy; it may have moments of nostalgia and melancholy. It is still amazing. It is anything but a mediocre existence where yesterday was the same as today and the day that follows is predictable.

Putting your money where your mouth is means feeding yourself. If you find that you are meeting a lot of people but nothing is happening the solution is probably not to meet more and more people. It may mean changing yourself in a way that can help you for life. You may need to reformat your mind, clean out the stupid thoughts, and overhaul your lifestyle.

You will never regret transformation. Just rediscover what it means to become a man. Ninety percent of your problems will go away at work, in relationships, and your quest to find a pack to run with.

That is the only thing society expects from you. It is not complicated. Be a man. Be the man you were created to be. If someone throws clothes into a washer they expect the clothes to come out clean. Not dry.

Most of the messages given to men today, however, seem to turn them into something else, women, androids, puppies, I don't know. But it is not to be men. This one answer solves all the social questions.

Say hi to someone or not? Be a man.

Stay home or go out? Be a man.

Text or call? Be a man.

Invite or not? Be a man.

Be offended or blow it off? Be a man.

Tell someone how you feel about them or be safe and talk about the seventy percent chance of rain this afternoon? Be a man.

Driving in your car, see someone you want to meet walking their dog on the street. Stop and put your hazards on and get out to talk to them or keep driving? Be a man.

Organize the happy hour or wait for someone else to do it? Be a man.

And this is the next thought of the social man: *The only thing I want is to show up and act like a man – nothing more.*

I am not going to pretend to know exactly what being a woman is all about but it will be the same on their side. If we are what we were created to be the social group falls into place. We were already created for it for society.

# 10

# The Thoughts That Should Never Be

*Give thanks twice a day that you have control over your mind.*

—Napoleon Hill

There are some thoughts you fill your mind with and there are some thoughts that should never be. I always believe it is more important to focus energy on putting the right thoughts in your mind than keeping the wrong ones out. Towards the evening of the day, however, there is one thought that seems to creep into the mind like a *cucaracha* at night looking for kitchen floor crumbs. You got to squash that thought without hesitation. Don't let the bugs wander around your mind.

I used to battle with that thought, the thought that should never be. I fought with it until Paris. There, in France, I realized how useless that thought was. I made a commitment to live a life where that thought-that-should-never-be had no place.

I stepped off the train and set foot in the most romantic city in the world. I was for the first time in the capital of France. I rolled my bags a few blocks and settled into my hostel. I went for my usual three-mile exploration jog, something I do on arriving to a new city or place. It puts me in a great mood and gives me an idea for what's going on in the area. Those are two important steps for creating a great adventure. After I showered and smelled fresh (step three) I was ready to take on the city.

I decided on a fun bar close to where I was staying. It was a busy place, warm with travelers mostly around my age.

I ordered my food, sat down and let the travel adrenaline wind down. I never really make detailed plans before visiting a city so I had to figure out what I was going to do there. I looked around me and saw friends clinking beers, couples gazing at each other over a glass of wine. Paris had good vibes.

Then it suddenly hit me, that dumb thought that comes to mind when I have nothing on my mind. *Why am I alone?* I was the only person in this entire bar who was not with somebody. And then that thought grew into another thought that was outright weird: *Is there something wrong with me?*

Of course there were reasons I was alone: my friends were all tied up and couldn't go on vacation with me, I decided to come to Paris with two weeks' notice, which certainly didn't help in engaging a travel companion. Probably most significant, I hadn't invited anybody to come to France with me anyway and if you don't invite anyone people normally don't come. However, at that moment the feelings were doing the thinking and they wanted to know, *Why is it just me?*

It is a natural question. I know it is a question a lot of people ask; but sometimes the natural question is not always the right question. The social man never asks why he is alone. Why ask a question when you have no control over the answer? Why I am alone is outside my control. I can't force anyone to travel to Paris with me.

Maybe at times we prefer those fantastical questions precisely because the answers are outside our control. We have no responsibility to act.

*When am I going to get my dream job?*

*When will I find someone special?*

*Why am I not yet married?*

There really is no response or at least no response that matters. None of the answers are in our control.

It is much more difficult to ask the real questions that have real, tangible answers:

*Why did I not wake up on time this morning?*

*Why did I swallow four Car Bombs last night?*

*Why did I not smile and say hello to that stranger standing in line with me?*

*Why do I allow myself to get defensive and annoyed over what people say?*

*Why do I stay in watching TV instead of joining the softball team and meeting new people?*

These are the questions I need to ask myself. I have near absolute power over the answers. I can determine the outcome.

I *can* wake up earlier to do meditation and start the day with positive thoughts.

I *can* turn my phone off and say hello.

I *can* get out of my loungewear, drive ten minutes to the art studio and show up for the drawing class I have wanted to take.

I never ask why I am alone. I certainly don't ask why I'm not married. Finding companionship, marriage, and even staying married is something I do not have control over. I will never worry about them. The social man recognizes and accepts that people can join him or leave him and that is all outside his control.

## Some things are gifts

Companionship is a gift. Love is freely given. I do not have direct control over these things. Unless you're a dictator in a communist regime, you generally do not have control over other people.

Where two or more people come together free will is involved. Free will can never be fully explained. And that is what makes it free. You have free will and others have it too. You cannot control theirs. Asking why they make choices is pointless.

I can only ask what I am doing right now with the hundreds of opportunities over which I do have control. What am I doing in this very instant, 6:01 p.m., to become the ideal man I have in my vision? Which specific actions have I taken to get there?

You cannot control if you are surrounded with people you love. You cannot decide if you get a girlfriend or boyfriend. Even the serial daters among us cannot control with 100% certainty if we will go out with someone tonight and the most social man cannot say with certainty if any of the nine people he texted will join him for happy hour.

Someone always needs to say yes and even when the odds are in your favor and your lucky star is blinking, people will sometimes say no. And that is the excitement of it. You never know. Companionship in any shape or form is always a gift.

Every relationship is a mystery. Fortunately, I've realized I don't need to solve it. I do not even need to understand it. I do not need to know why "it didn't work out" or why someone is not interested or why nobody could make it out tonight.

My mentors, my learning, my convictions have already mapped out my course of action. That is the benefit of having someone who knows the way to guide you. You never have to ask why. Just follow the process.

All I need to do is put the effort forward. All I need is my "yes" every day at 5:05 a.m. in order to start the day and live well. My own yes to life is far more important than a thousand answers from other people.

I have the power to laugh, to resent or to love. I am blessed to live in a country with no hard social barriers and I can speak to whomever I want: men, women, rich or crazy rich. I have control over so many things. I can walk outside wearing sweatpants or a suit. I can eat Keto or I can eat Cheetos. Of all these decisions there is one that matters most. I can create love or wait around to receive it.

A mentor once told me that people never really get sad. They just get bored. What they really want is adventure. That is in everyone's power as well. You do not need a thousand dollars and a plane ticket to Ibiza for adventure. You can a make a trip to Target a social adventure if you want to. Adventure is always within grasp if you have a bit of courage.

It is not easy doing all these things, making decisions and following up on decisions with action. It is, however, infinitely easier than begging the skies to send down an answer for a question that you were never meant to ask.

In the first biblical story, the man Adam never asked for Eve. It was God's idea. God saw he was ready for it and he molded, created companionship, while Adam was simply doing what he was created to do. God is the author of life. Do what you should be doing and let God do what God does.

Seizing your area of control will do infinitely more for your social or romantic life than asking yourself the uncontrollable question, "Why am I alone?"

There is so much we can do. Why waste a single instant pondering about something you cannot?

Why waste even three seconds wondering why someone did not respond to your text message?

Why waste an ounce of emotion over whether or not someone says yes to going out tonight?

Why waste a single heartbeat wondering if somebody is "interested" or if they will swipe on you?

I think the greatest disappointment in the world is waiting for results in a situation over which you have no control. The most satisfying experience is to make an effort that has the possibility of producing something good in the world.

## Action takers smile more

Taking action makes us happy. Running the risk gives us something to live for. Doing something dangerous makes our heart beat again. Everything you need to do to feel alive is in your power. Reach out. Try. Change yourself. Share love. Show up in front of the world.

If you see someone you want to say hi to, stop your car, put your hazards on, get out and do it. You won't feel alone any longer.

I do not believe rejection exists; but if it did, it is still a little better than wondering, *What if?* Even feeling rejected is better than not feeling anything at all.

In my journey to being proactive, I quickly realized that the days I took action were the happiest days of the week. It did not matter the outcome of the action. It only mattered that I tried.

I applied for a better position. That felt good.

I said, "Good morning," to a stranger on the train. That was amazing.

We may or may not have been created to achieve the dream we have in mind. We definitely were not put here to be powerless sufferers incapable of taking action. We definitely were not made to just watch it float on by because we're scared of getting wet. Decide, move the feet, speak, encounter, that is the human way.

Barcelona taught me that. On one European trip I was walking along Barcelona beach. After I'd had sufficient me time I decided I wanted to meet some people.

I met some friendly Germans at the outdoor beach gym. We did some pull-ups and made Instagram videos.

I went by the water to tan and said hello to a Spanish girl coming out of the water. She gave me a short stare and looked away. OK, maybe she just wasn't in the mood to socialize.

I started talking to an Irish traveler set up beside me instead and we exchanged travel tips and itineraries.

A few yards down I met some Italians competing in an informal beach volleyball tournament. They said yes to me and I spent the next three hours dominating the courts with them.

Then I went walking along the ocean looking for some coffee. I saw a young French woman with short, blonde hair carrying a yoga mat towards me. *Cool, a fellow yogi*, I thought to myself. I said, "Hi," and we chatted for a minute talking about what brought us to Spain. She seemed interesting; I wanted to invite her to grab coffee with me. For some reason I didn't. I just said, "Goodbye." That was still better than doing nothing though.

Later that evening, when I thought about my adventures, I did not think of the people who did not want to hang out with me. I did think of the people who did. I thought a lot about the person who I didn't even invite to have coffee with me. "What if..." I could have gotten to know a really interesting person. It is always the "what if" that keeps us up at night, never the "no's". The "no's" you heard will fall out of your mind and melt into the pillow and you will sleep fine. The "what if" has you binge watching a mini series and eating ice cream until your mind is too exhausted to think about anything.

I learned somewhat late in life that it is not failure that makes us sad. Sometimes days filled with the most failures and rejection were the most fulfilled. It is fear that makes us miserable. Doing nothing when we could have done something is the first step to living a life of regret. *What if* will always be more painful than *I tried*.

**Hi, you're pretty**

Coming back to the Parisian bar where I sat alone. I stared at my cheese thinking these things over.

Just then, a nice young lady crossed in front of me and grabbed a table in the corner. I looked twice. I was suddenly curious. *Maybe I'll talk to her.* She seemed about my age, probably younger. *Maybe we'll have something common. Maybe she doesn't even speak English; this is France, after all. Maybe her boyfriend is outside and going to come in any minute. Maybe I'll just say, "Hi," and go back to my cheese.*

There were so many thoughts. I had to regroup, however, and remember that a "maybe" has no value. All that matters was if I would act on my raw inspiration of the moment.

The alternative was to sit there staring at my phone tethered to the sluggish Wi-Fi. It's funny how if I stared at a 3.5-inch screen all day growing up in the '90s I would have been a complete nerd or just weird. Somehow, today it is the norm.

I was excited to be in Paris. I wanted to share that excitement with someone even if just for a few seconds. Somewhere inside me there was also a self-centered coward worried about what people think of me. The good side won, however, and I got up to say hello to her.

It turned out she was Italian, a solo traveler, also a first-timer in Paris. I spoke Italian so we had at least one thing in common. Really, language matters little though. If you really want to get to know someone or spend time with them you will find a way to let them know.

After introductions I went back to my table to grab my cheese and sat there having dinner with her. It turned out we had a lot in common. We both were fans of Jacque Louise David and Neoclassicism. We both wanted to see the Louvre, Eiffel Tower and Montmartre. More importantly, we both were seasoned walkers, a real deal-breaker for exploring European cities.

The next day we started early, had coffee together, and then explored Paris for an entire day. Suddenly, I wasn't alone anymore. I did not have to answer that question. I just had to take action where I could. The Italian was amazing, full of meaningful conversation and the best travel companion I could ask for. We extended our time together until I ran the risk of missing my flight back to the US that evening.

Standing in a busy stairwell of the Louvre, we said goodbye. My way was down, hers was up. Then I was about to turn and walk away and she came forward to embrace me one more time, knowing that odds were we would never see each other again. It was a good day.

Those who are convinced of their course of action never ask why. Why is a word for the uncertain. When you are absolutely convinced you are on the right path in life, you don't even bother looking at results. If your course of action is right then the right results will follow sooner or later.

If you are absolutely sure it is water that is coming out of the hose you do not need to sit there for 20 minutes wondering if the basil plant on your porch will grow. The plant will grow. You put the right action forth though. You watered it. That is what mattered.

When I was a lost child, I asked why. But now I know that I am already doing everything possible to get to where I need to go. I still search and learn but I never doubt my actions for today. My seasoned mentor is guiding me and I have complete faith in him. I have thought deeply about who I am and why I am here. I know my purpose. I seize every opportunity I have to act and I am proud to say that the sin of deferral rarely shows up in Confession. Yes, now I can stop asking why and simply live.

When that happens, your day is full of meeting amazing people and you do not even have time to think of marriage or whatever happened to that guy or why that girl is not responding. So and so never hangs out anymore. Who cares? You know where you are going.

Some people ask God to take action while they themselves worry about results. Others take action and let God worry about results. I no longer ask why I am alone at the moment and only ask how much love I am giving to the world. Companionship is a result well beyond our power. I can never guarantee I will be spending time with someone, but in the meantime the whole world is mine for the taking.

The thought that should never be: *Why am I alone?* If I have time to ask that question I have time to take action.

# The Second Beginning

Being social is a way of life connected to people. Those connections may become acquaintances. They may become friends. One of them may become your husband or wife. They may just make you laugh in the moment and then never be seen again. It does not really matter because being social is not about being popular, having a database of friends, or standing in the limelight of every party. All that may happen, but it is not about that. You do not care how people respond to you. Being social is about how you want to show up to the world. You can show up afraid of rejection or you can show up unafraid.

Social is a lifestyle I pursue because it is one I enjoy. If I'm out having coffee Saturday morning and I see a group of nurses wearing scrubs with my hospital's logo coming off the night shift to grab brunch, I like to meet them and say hi.

If I'm out for a jog and see someone running my pace I like to say hi and maybe even jog with them.

Sometimes I get out of the office after a long day and would like to have a non-work-related conversation with someone on the metro ride home.

In all those moments and more I do not want a fear of rejection or shyness of strangers or whatever you call it holding me back. I want to be free. I want social freedom.

From having to move a lot and start over, I used to think I did not have a lot of people in my life. Then I realized that my life is full of great people. In each moment the people in my life are not just my family, friends distant or near, or professional connections I'll see on Monday. The people in my life are whoever is standing, sitting around me at any given moment of the day. It is all the people I see during the day. Being social is about expanding my horizons to see that and following the feeling to encounter them. The people in my life are the ones God has placed in my immediate surroundings.

I may spend an entire weekend alone in coffee shops working on projects. I may be surrounded with friends at a weekend beach house. The circumstances do not matter. The way people respond to me does not matter. My actions do. I do not have to say hello to everyone. I do not have to make friends with the entire world. I only need to be faithful to the urge within to encounter the people I see. That feeling is a God-given urge to connect with the rest of humanity. To ignore it is to ignore a gift.

Throughout my journey I have thought that personality, temperament, and social virtues like confidence and charm are what make us more or less social. It really has little to do with that, though, and is much simpler than all of that. I do not have to "get good with people" or learn a series of social techniques. I do not have to know how to do the confident handshake or spend energy feigning interest in someone talk about their glamping trip last weekend. All that matters is that I create the right thoughts. Wash the mind. Clean out the presumptions about myself, others, and the world. I have learned that in the end, rejection does not exist. Nobody rejects me. I only reject myself in my mind. Then, others simply agree with me.

Create the right thoughts and being social just happens; it becomes irresistible and compelling. My social life is built on thoughts not on some special talent I was born with. There are probably a thousand techniques to overcome fear of rejection, but I can't think of a better one for the introvert mind. Rejection is born in the mind and it is in the mind that it dies. I only need to think well and gain absolute control over my mind.

Start thinking well, or, if you can, stop thinking all together. Take control of your mind and everything else will follow.

**You can say hi at the museum**

# The Social Introvert Cheat Sheet

Things to remember

1. Good thoughts create good actions (like saying "Hi" to people).

2. Stop trying to be social, just think amazing and your thoughts will do the work.

3. Everything in your mind manifests in your attitude, action, or energy. Be careful about what is in your mind.

4. Fall in love with the now and stop thinking about what you are going to say next.

5. Thoughts are superpowers. They can do you a lot of good or a lot of harm.

Things you can think:

1. The world loves me and is waiting to meet me.

2. I am here to give and need nothing from anyone.

3. I live in the world with a purpose. That purpose is more important than anything that could happen to me today. It is bigger than rejection.

Good words to describe your feelings:

1. Tremendous

2. Awesome

3. Epic

4. Fulfilled

5. Love for the present

6. Good about the future

7. Thankful for the past

8. At peace

Times you can check your thoughts:

1. Every morning

2. Lunch break

3. Before bed

4. Before social situations

# Notes:

**For a discussion on the nice guy:**
Glover, Robert A. *No More Mr. Nice Guy: a Proven Plan for Getting What You Want in Love, Sex, and Life.* Running Press, 2017.

**This book got me *thinking*:**
Allen, James. *As a Man Thinketh.* Facsimile Publisher, 2017.

**Rules 2 and 6 influenced how I see myself and the world:**
Peterson, Jordan B., Ethan Van Sciver, and Norman Doidge. *12 Rules for Life: an Antidote to Chaos.* Toronto: Vintage Canada, 2020.

**If wealth begins with the mind, would good things begin there, as well?**
Hill, Napoleon. *Think and Grow Rich.* New Delhi: GenNext Publication, 2019.

**Sometimes we introverts complicate things but this read simplifies man behavior:**
Deida, David. *The Way of the Superior Man a Spiritual Guide to Mastering the Challenges of Women, Work and Sexual Desire.* Boulder: Sounds True, 2017.

**Introverts, don't let your mind control you:**
Tolle, Eckhart. *The Power of Now: a Guide to Spiritual Enlightenment.* Sydney, NSW: Hachette Australia, 2018.

**I went to a primary source for the chivalry discussion:**
Charny, Geoffroi de, Richard W. Kaeuper, and Elspeth Kennedy. *A Knights Own Book of Chivalry Geoffroi De Charny.* Philadelphia (Pa.): University of Pennsylvania Press, 2005.

**Don't let your tech keep you from making friends:**
Eyal, Nir. *Indistractable: How to Control Your Attention and Choose Your Life.* Dallas, (Tx.): BenBella Books, 2019

**I was thinking, if we're watching this porn are we really living the dream?**
https://medium.com/@Strange_bt_True/how-big-is-the-porn-industry-fbc1ac78091b

**Jordan Peterson, again, on why weak men can't be virtuous:**
https://www.youtube.com/watch?v=bWYrAU5mmXE

# About the Author

John spent fifteen years in a Catholic seminary building meaningful communities while learning the ascetic life of meditation and silence.

Upon discerning out of the seminary, he continued his passion for both quiet and community. While saying hi around the world he developed the *Always Say Hi* lifestyle by which introverts can avoid "social burnout" and effortlessly create memorable experiences with people in their everyday commute, routine, and activities.

Today, he lives in Houston, Texas where he plans hiking trips and partners with busy professionals who want to make the world a friendlier place one hi at a time.

Connect or just say hi at:
Instagram @always.say.hi
Twitter @alwayssayhibook
alwayssayhi.com

Made in the USA
Columbia, SC
06 November 2020

24081151R10089